P9-AZU-369

The Testing Gap

Scientific Trials of Test-Driven
School Accountability Systems
for Excellence and Equity

A volume in
Research in Educational Policy: Local, National, and Global Perspectives
Kenneth K. Wong, *Series Editor*

The Testing Gap

Scientific Trials of Test-Driven School Accountability Systems for Excellence and Equity

by

Jaekyung Lee

INFORMATION AGE PUBLISHING

Charlotte, NC • www.infoagepub.com

Library of Congress Cataloging-in-Publication Data

Lee, Jaekyung.
  The testing gap : scientific trials of test-driven school accountability
systems for excellence and equity / by Jaekyung Lee.
      p. cm. – (Research in educational policy: local, national and
global perspectives)
  Includes bibliographical references.
  ISBN 978-1-59311-748-1 (pbk.) – ISBN 978-1-59311-749-8 (hardcover)
  1. Educational accountability–United States. 2. National Assessment of
Educational Progress (Project) 3. United States. No Child Left Behind Act
of 2001. I. Title.
  LB2806.22.L43 2007
  379.1'58–dc22

                                                              2007010806

Printed in the United States of America

To My Mother

CONTENTS

PART I

Policy, Research and Practice of Test-Driven External Accountability

PART II

Impact of NCLB and State Accountability
on the Achievement Gap

PART III

Transforming the Future of Educational Accountability System

PART IV

Appendices

PREFACE

Student performance and school accountability have been keywords in educational policy discourse in the past two decades as policymakers consider what actions to take to improve academic achievement for all students. There was a wake-up call for public school reform to tackle the alleged mediocrity of American education in the midst of an international brain race, causing the focus of educational policy goals to shift from equity to excellence, and the level of expected student performance from minimum competency to proficiency. Newly adopted curriculum standards and high-stakes testing have functioned as the linchpin of this policy shift. This policy shift culminated in the most recent federal educational policy initiative, the *No Child Left Behind Act* (NCLB).

NCLB requires yearly progress of all groups of students toward the state proficiency levels in reading and mathematics. What percentage of schools and their kids across the nation will meet desired performance standards by 2014, the deadline for achieving the laudable goal of 100 percent proficiency? Although it is hard to project the future outcome of the test-driven external school accountability policies under NCLB, continuing the trends of the first several years since NCLB's inception may end up leaving many disadvantaged minority students far behind with little opportunity to meet the 2014 target. It is possible under the current system of accountability that the state assessment may continue to give a false impression of progress, shortchanging our children and encouraging more investment into the policy.

NCLB has promoted controversies about whether external, test-driven accountability policy enhances or hinders equity. While concerns about the erosion of educational equity have been raised, this policy debate tends to polarize between the extremes. While NCLB builds upon the alleged success of states that had adopted accountability policies prior to NCLB—so-called first-generation accountability states such as Florida, North Carolina

The Testing Gap, pages ix–xi

and Texas—assessing its full impact requires a more rigorous scrutiny of new evidence from all states, including second-generation states, and based on data from an independent national assessment as well as states' own assessment results. It is time to give an in-depth look into reading and math achievement trends across the nation and states before and after NCLB to explore the policy impact on closing the achievement gap among racial and social groups.

The objective of this book is to advance our understanding of the design, implementation and evaluation of test-driven external accountability policies for improving both academic excellence and equity. This book provides new insights into debates about the efficacy of high-stakes testing through critical synthesis of previous studies and through systematic analysis of the achievement gap trends over the past 15 years. The core findings have implications for contemporary national and state policy efforts, as mandated by NCLB, to close the achievement gap. The book alerts readers to scientific, institutional and technical threats to the current test-driven school accountability system, and possible consequences if we fail to counteract those threats and continue the current policy course with underfunded mandates and an over-reliance on testing and sanctions.

The author is very grateful to numerous individuals for their assistance with this book. Particularly, Part II of this book is based on my earlier report commissioned by Harvard University Civil Rights Project. Special thanks go to Gail Sunderman and Gary Orfield who contributed greatly to reviewing and editing this part. I am also very grateful to external reviewers, Doug Harris, Gene Glass, and Robert Linn who provided invaluable comments and suggestions on an earlier draft of Part II. Further, I deeply appreciate constructive feedback given by two anonymous reviewers of the earlier version of my entire book manuscript.

I am also very grateful to my former teachers at the University of Chicago, including Ken Wong, Tony Bryk, Bob Dreeben, Ben Wright, and Larry Hedges. They all have helped me develop my thinking and analytical skills. Particularly, Dr. Wong who is the editor of this book series gave me continuing encouragement and support for this publication. I also benefited from working with my colleagues, including Walter McIntire and Ted Coladarci at the University of Maine, and Jeremy Finn at the University at Buffalo. I also thank generous administrative support from my former and current schools.

My writing of this book has benefited greatly from several research projects that I have conducted in the past 10 years. Previous studies that have become the foundation of this book have been sponsored by the National Academy of Education/Spencer Foundation Postdoctoral Fellowship, the U.S. Department of Education NAEP Secondary Analysis Grant, the American Educational Research Association Research Grant, and the

National Science Foundation Systemic Initiatives Research Grant. Through the course of these projects, I appreciate assistance from graduate students: Steve McVeit, Yuhong Sun, and Mary Anne (University of Maine); Eben Schwartz, Jie Wang, Jeff Fox, and Greg Beehler (University at Buffalo). Any opinions, conclusions and recommendations in this book are solely mine.

Finally, I am deeply indebted to my mother who has more than happily sacrificed her life for me. Without her care, support and encouragement, I could not have come to this point in my professional life. Splendid child achievement is never preceded by anything less than splendid parenting. Although this book is only a modest achievement of mine, I proudly dedicate it to my mother.

INTRODUCTION

AIM HIGH, HIT HIGH?

Since *A Nation at Risk* (NCEE, 1983) gave a wake-up call to address alleged educational mediocrity in the American public school system, many states jumped on the bandwagon of a standards-raising education reform movement. During this period, the focus of educational policy shifted from equity to excellence, and the level of the performance standard was raised from minimum competency to proficiency. Accountability has become the linchpin of this policy shift. One significant accountability milestone took place in 1989 at the National Education Summit of state governors to establish education goals for 2000 (Walberg, 2003). This Goals 2000 program was enacted into law in 1994, pushing for national standards and assessments (Ravitch, 1995). At the same time, the Improving America's Schools Act of 1994 (IASA), the law that reauthorizes the Elementary and Secondary Education Act of 1965 (ESEA), reinforced the performance-based accountability movement for Title I schools. During the last decade, many states have raised performance standards for students and used high-stakes testing to measure and improve the quality of public education. The culmination of this policy shift is seen in the most recent federal educational policy initiative, the No Child Left Behind Act of 2001 (NCLB), which is aimed at accomplishing high academic standards for all students and closing their achievement gaps.

Achievement gaps constitute important barometers in educational and social progress. Since the Coleman Report in the 1960s brought attention to racial inequity in student outcomes, the achievement gap between White and minority students has raised a multitude of concerns and resulted in a significant body of empirical research (Coleman et al., 1966; Jencks & Phillips, 1998; Lee, 2002). The achievement gap can be viewed

The Testing Gap, pages 1–23
Copyright © 2007 by Information Age Publishing
All rights of reproduction in any form reserved.

and assessed from both excellence and equity perspectives. Equity concerns relative achievement of different groups of students and schools. The National Assessment of Educational Progress (NAEP), the so-called nation's report card of student achievement, provides information on the achievement gaps among different racial and socioeconomic groups in core academic subjects. For example, there is a documented achievement gap in mathematics between White students and minority students in the U.S., particularly socio-economically disadvantaged Black and Hispanic students; an average Black high school graduate's standardized math test score can be as low as that of an average White 8th grader (Lee, 2004c).

No matter how much this kind of relative gap among different racial and socioeconomic groups has been narrowed, some disadvantaged minority students' performance level still may not be acceptable. For example, about 70 percent of 12th grade Black students perform below the basic achievement level in mathematics. The investigation of achievement gaps from an excellence perspective that concerns primarily how well students perform against a certain level of achievement deemed adequate. This adds a new dimension of gap relative to adequate performance, thereby removing the possibility of lowering the achievement of the higher performing group in order to close the relative gap.

NCLB provides new opportunities and challenges for states to advance the goal of closing the achievement gap. Under NCLB, States have until the 2005–06 school year to implement aligned, annual reading or language arts and mathematics assessments in each grade, 3 through 8, and at the high school level (at least once annually in grades 10 through 12). It relies on high-stakes testing to ensure that schools make Adequate Yearly Progress (AYP) toward the goal of 100% proficiency for all students by 2014. One crucial component of the requirement is that districts and schools must reach annual achievement goals not only overall but also for specified subgroups of students including students from major racial and ethnic groups, economically disadvantaged students, students with disabilities, and students with limited English proficiency. Researchers and educators have raised concerns about the negative consequences of NCLB's test-based accountability and its uniform performance requirement, including its potential to perpetuate or exacerbate existing racial, economic, or geographic inequalities among schools and students (Kim & Sunderman, 2004; Lee, 2003; Lee, 2004b; Linn, 2003). Also, education advocates, state education officials, and some members of Congress were concerned about unfunded NCLB mandates and called for more serious federal efforts to accomplish the original intent of the law (Mathis, 2003; NAACP, 2005; NSBA, 2006).[1] Many disadvantaged high-minority schools across the nation are highly unlikely to reach the current AYP goal under NCLB unless we lower the target achievement level or extend the timeline to reach the level.

Current controversies about high-stakes testing and test-driven school accountability raise many outstanding questions. To better understand the impact of educational accountability policy on academic excellence and equity, it is necessary to address the following questions: Why did states shift the focus of their accountability practices from school inputs to student outcomes? If states did so because of an alleged public school failure, did new state accountability policy bring about any changes in educational resource allocations? If their assertion of failure is misguided, what are the consequences of state policy shifts for student outcomes? Did performance-driven accountability bypass the issue of disparities in schooling resources and opportunities for low-income, minority students? If states ignored equity issues, were they still able to narrow the persistent racial and socioeconomic achievement gaps?

STANDARDS-BASED EDUCATION REFORM: THE NATIONAL CRUSADE FOR EXCELLENCE AND EQUITY

This standards-based education reform and test-driven school accountability movement in the U.S. was facilitated by international brain race and comparison of test results (D. Baker, 2003; Husén & Tuijnman, 1994; Lee, 2001). Findings from Trends in International Math and Science Study (TIMSS) showed that the U.S fell short of achieving the national goal of being first in the world in mathematics and science achievement by the year 2000 (NCES, 1996). The TIMSS curriculum study also pointed out the prevailing problem of current U.S. curricula, that is, "a mile wide and an inch deep" characterizing broad, superficial coverage of many topics (Schmidt et al., 1997). Indeed, American education has been criticized for a lack of common rigorous curriculum standards that define what all students should know and be able to do. *A Nation at Risk* (NCEE, 1983) report noted that "we tend to express our educational standards and expectations largely in terms of 'minimum' requirements.... In some metropolitan areas basic literacy has become the goal rather than the starting point." Once President George W. Bush decried this problem in a speech calling for school accountability reform (Jan. 8, 2004): "We are challenging the soft bigotry of low expectations. Despite the rhetoric, the key policy challenge in U.S. education, a culturally diverse and politically decentralized country, was to develop a systemic reform model, that is, "a uniquely American adaptation of the education policies and structures of many of the world's highly developed nations" (O'Day & Smith, 1993, p. 252).

The hallmark of education reform during the last two decades can be labeled standards-based or systemic (Porter, 2003; Ravitch, 1995). Standards have been at the center of education reform. The key idea is to have a coherent state education policy system aimed at high academic standards for all students, specifying what the students should know and be able to do in core subject areas (Smith & O'Day, 1991). While the various levels of the school system would have particular administrative responsibility for the activities of their own level and for those of their subordinate levels, it was assumed that the nation-state has the authority to establish content and performance standards nationwide or statewide and to hold local districts or schools accountable for outcomes. This systemic school reform considers the effects of change on the total school system over a sustained period of time, and thus it is distinctive in terms of the scale and nature of program operation.

Therefore, high-stakes testing and test-driven accountability policy may be better understood in light of broader standards-based state education reform movement. While the origin of public high-stakes testing dates as far back as the 2nd century B.C., when civil service exams were used by the Han emperors of China (206 B.C. to A.D. 220), modern external examinations have grown as instruments of control over educational systems in many countries (Eckstein & Noah, 1993). High-stakes tests in American school systems are relatively recent and they are embedded in national educational and social contexts. It has been argued that the United States is one of the rare developed countries without a high-stakes exit exam for high school students and thus American students do not work as hard as their counterparts in higher-performing countries (Bishop, 2001; Tomlinson & Cross, 1991). While states relied more on basic skills tests in the 1970s, *A Nation at Risk* (NCEE, 1983) called for an end to the minimum competency testing movement (Amrein & Berliner, 2002). The focus of high-stakes testing policy shifted from minimum competency to proficiency, and increasing numbers of states held schools accountable for these results during the last two decades.

What is the role of educational standards and testing for accountability, excellence and equity? Standards function as a model or goal of education (e.g., Goals 2000). They also function as a criterion or yardstick, producing a measure of progress toward the goal (e.g., NCLB Adequate Yearly Progress measure). There are three major types of educational standards:

1. Content standards: What students should know and be able to do (e.g., National Council of Teachers of Mathematics (NCTM) curriculum standards, Maine Learning Results)

2. Performance standards: Degree of mastery or levels of achievement (e.g., NAEP achievement levels including Basic, Proficient, and Advanced)

3. Opportunity-to-learn standards or school delivery standards: Availability of programs, staff, and resources for students to meet the content and performance standards (e.g., school funding adequacy, teacher qualification standards).

How did educational accountability reform advance the goals of academic excellence and equity? Figure 1 highlights the interconnections among policy instruments; standards are used to support and advance these three goals. New curriculum, textbooks, and assessment are tools that help connect the standards to underlying goals including academic excellence and equity. A school accountability system using performance reporting, rewards and sanctions take a step further to ensure that schools successfully translate these standards into desired results for all students.

The evaluation of standards-based education reform depends on the criteria used. For example, if we take course enrollments and instructional time in core subjects as the evaluative criteria, the implementation of standards-raising reform can be viewed as successful. On the other hand, if we base our final judgments on instructional practices and student outcomes, the ultimate effect of reform remains dubious. Content-driven systemic school reform emerged during the last decade as a major policy alternative in the United States (Smith & O'Day, 1991). This is in part due to the limits of the past education policy to bring about instructional change at the classroom level. Indeed, previous studies of curriculum reform find that new ideas hardly take root in the practice of teachers because those ideas are not reinforced in the immediate work environment of students and teachers (Elmore, 1995). A remarkable mélange of traditional and progressive approaches to instruction has been noted: many teachers tend to construct hybrids of particular progressive practices grafted onto what they ordinarily did in the classroom (Cohen, 1990; Cuban, 1984). This tendency has been reinforced by state testing programs that were designed to insure a minimum level of learning.

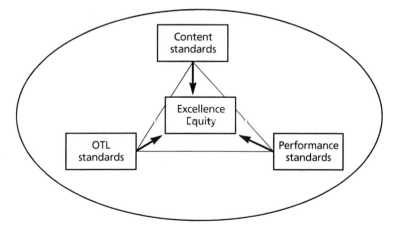

Figure 1.   The Role of Educational Standards for Academic Excellence and Equity.

To address these deficiencies in educational policy, state policymakers proposed reform policies intended to significantly upgrade the quality of the curriculum and instruction delivered to all children. Major reforms include the establishment of state curriculum frameworks, the development of student assessments and the adoption of new textbooks tied to the curriculum frameworks. However, standards are still in flux under NCLB. Recent study of NCLB implementation shows that states continue to revise content standards (American Institutes for Research, 2006). Since 2002, 29 states have either adopted or revised their state standards in ELA and 28 states in math. States also continue to amend their assessments and AYP plan.

Student-centered instructional practices with a strong emphasis on higher-order thinking skills are considered positive signs of this policy implementation. Lee (1998b) finds that content-driven state policies have great influences on instruction at the school level, and are associated with desired instructional practices at the classroom level. Lubienski (2006) found significant positive relationships between reform-oriented practices (teacher emphasis on non-number mathematics strands, collaborative problem solving etc.) and 4th-grade student achievement. Lee (2004a) also found a positive relationship between reform-oriented practices and 8th-grade student achievement.

Despite relatively widespread consensus on the rationale of systemic school reform that seeks to achieve more rigorous content and performance standards for all students in core subjects, state policy approaches to helping schools achieve this goal tend to divide between a primary emphasis on input guarantees as a mechanism for achieving equal access to learning and a primary emphasis on performance guarantees as a means for achieving desired results (Elmore & Fuhrman, 1995). The advocates of opportunity-to-learn (OTL) standards argue that every student must have equal access to high-quality learning by specifying key inputs (per-pupil spending, textbooks, teacher training, and the like) in the form of binding standards. The achievement gaps among racial and socioeconomic groups have been found to be relatively small in states with more equitable distribution of school resources and classroom OTL (Wong & Lee, 1998).

In contrast, the critics of OTL standards argue that input standards of any kind create constraints on how educators respond to the learning problems of students. The advocates of performance standards and test-driven accountability claim that lifting regulations on school inputs and practices but holding schools accountable for desired results will provide incentives for schools to run more efficiently and maximize performance outcomes as measured by test scores.

While the critics of OTL standards argue that holding schools and students accountable for performance creates incentives for schools to find out which practices work most effectively, there is no guarantee that performance measures automatically lead to increased equality in the distribution of student learning (O'Day & Smith, 1993). O'Day and Smith (1993) point out the inherent problems with a performance-based accountability model with clearly defined outcome standards for schools, the approach most often suggested in current policy proposals:

> Indeed, a solely performance-based strategy might be likened to closing the barn door after the horse is stolen. We know that many schools simply do not have the resources to provide the level of opportunity necessary for their students. We do not need to wait until we have clear outcome documentation of failure before addressing obvious problems. Moreover, once failure is noted, there is no assurance in this model that schools of the poor would have the knowledge or other capacity to improve, nor is there any mechanism to stimulate outside assistance. (pp. 270–271)

Indeed, the two approaches are not mutually exclusive, and combining them could be the most successful path. Bartman (2002) argued that most successful reforms have relied on assessments, disaggregating data by race, and investing in teacher training. Bartman observed that this kind of success can be seen in combined judicial and legislative efforts in Kentucky and Texas, which have been successful in increasing access to quality education for minority students. Valencia et al. (2004) also argued that to shift from an "inputs-driven" to a "results-driven" accountability model is misguided; rather, a tripartite structure with equal attention to input, process, and output is needed. Fiske and Ladd (2000), in their analysis of the implementation of market-oriented educational reform in New Zealand, proposed that there is a need to delineate the linkages in a "tight-loose-tight" governance system.[2]

Lee (2006b) shows that the effects of accountability on academic achievement are moderated by the availability of school resources. As the researchers whose studies showed the positive impact of accountability on achievement often acknowledged, lower class sizes and increased, more equitable funding in Texas have created a context in which the accountability system could increase academic excellence and equity (Grissmer, Flanagan, Kawata, & Williamson, 2000; Skrla, Scheurich, Johnson, & Koschoreck, 2004). Equity concerns can be better addressed from top down by a higher level of government that has both political willingness and financial capacity to reallocate resources (Peterson, 1981; Wong, 1994). On the other end, academic excellence should be pursued from bottom up, at the lowest level of the school system, that is, at the classroom level, as teachers know best about individual students and thus probably the most appropriate teaching decisions and practices can be made at that level. However, this approach will not work effectively if the process of schooling that transforms educational inputs into outcomes is treated simply as a black box or relegated entirely to professional judgment without external support and a mechanism of accountability. Accountability must be informed by information on effective instructional practices (Cohen, Raudenbush, & Ball, 2003; Raudenbush, 2004).

THEORY IN ACTION: HOW ACCOUNTABILITY WORKS FOR EXCELLENCE AND EQUITY

Accountability often has multiple meanings and purposes, and there are several models of educational accountability (see Adams & Kirst, 1999; Darling-Hammond, 1989; Linn, 2003). The issue of who holds whom accountable and for what purpose has been contentious in the history of educational accountability (Dorn, 1998). Despite the historical debate, an accountability model that is performance-driven, test-driven, measurable, and statistical in nature came to dominate current policy and practice. The logic of performance-driven accountability policy appears to draw upon rationalistic and behavioristic views of human behavior by positing that holding schools, teachers, and students accountable for academic performance, with incentives provided (i.e., rewards and sanctions), will inform, motivate, and reorient the behavior of schooling agents toward the goal (Benveniste, 1985; Wise, 1979; also see Rowan & Miskel, 1999; Shafritz & Ott, 2001, for more general organizational theories on these issues). Critics such as Elmore (2002) point out that the working theory behind test-based accountability system is fatally simple:

> Attaching stakes to test scores is supposed to create incentives for students and teachers to work harder and for school and district administrators to do a better job of monitoring their performance.... In fact, this is a naïve view of what it takes to improve student learning. Fundamentally, *internal* accountability must precede *external* accountability. A school's ability to make improvements has to do with the beliefs and practices that people in the organization share, not with the kind of information they receive about their performance. Low-performing schools aren't coherent enough to respond to external demands for accountability.... Most high-performing schools simply reflect the social capital of the students (they are primarily schools with students of high socioeconomic status), rather than the internal capacity of the students themselves. Most low-performing schools cannot rely on the social capital of students and families and instead must rely on their organizational capacity. With little or no investment in capacity, low-performing schools get worse relative to high-performing schools. (pp. 3–4)

The current federal school accountability policy fails to reflect the institutional realities of accountability in states, districts, and schools. Further, its provisions are considerably at odds with the technical realities of test-based accountability. Then, why did this idea of test-driven or performance-based accountability become so popular among educational policymakers across the nation and states? According to Elmore (2002), the idea of performance-based accountability was introduced in the mid 1980s by the National Governors Association, led by Bill Clinton and it took the form of what was then called the "horse trade": states would grant schools and districts more flexibility in return for more accountability for academic performance. It was appealing in principle since governors and state legislators could take credit for improving schools without committing themselves to serious increases in funding.

Educational reform policies that raise standards were designed to intensify, rather than to replace, preexisting educational efforts and were popular with state legislators because they held out the hope of greater cost-effectiveness (Berliner & Biddle, 1995). States that raised performance standards without corresponding attention to fiscal capacity and affordability created a greater need for support and assistance and were more likely to dismiss past policies as failures and switch to allegedly more cost-effective accountability policies. The cost of test-based accountability was reportedly so small relative to the cost of other educational programs (such as class size reduction) (Hoxby, 2002); the cost of paying for tests, publishing results and writing and publishing the standards on which the tests are graded, is about $5 per student on average. This estimate, however, included only the most basic part of an accountability system. Further studies are needed to address the cost of monitoring, identifying, assisting, rewarding, and/or punishing the target population of accountability according to their test results and other related information.

If states jumped on the bandwagon of accountability for the reasons of lower cost and the prospect of greater effectiveness, it also may have put many schools at risk by making them fall into the trap of increased control in return for results (states could blame the victim for poor school performance and then take over schools). A similar type of policy shift was noted in the past when minimum competency testing allegedly shifted the burden of attaining satisfactory results from the state to the individual (Cohen & Haney, 1980). But this time states tended to set higher standards for all students and to hold schools, rather than individuals, accountable for the results.

The research findings on the effects of high-stakes testing on improving academic performance have been mixed, generating controversy over the policy's usefulness (Amrein & Berliner, 2002; Carnoy & Loeb, 2002; Grissmer & Flanagan, 1998; Hanushek & Raymond, 2004; Lee, 2006a; Lee & Wong, 2004; Nichols, Glass, & Berliner, 2006; Raymond & Hanushek, 2003; West & Peterson, 2005).[3] The case that drew the most attention was Texas, where the evidence on the impact of high-stakes testing was highly contested (Carnoy, Loeb, & Smith, 2001; Grissmer & Flanagan, 1998; Grissmer, Flanagan, Kawata, & Williamson, 2000; Haney, 2000; Skrla et al., 2004; Valencia et al., 2004).

There are controversies about whether external, performance-driven accountability policy enhances or hinders equity. On the one hand, raising performance standards and measuring the results with high-stakes testing may contribute to narrowing the achievement gaps by motivating lower-achieving, disadvantaged minority students and their schools to improve academic achievement at a greater rate than that of their higher-achieving, less disadvantaged counterparts. Case studies have shown some exemplar districts and schools to have made significant academic progress on standardized test measures by capitalizing on accountability policies to improve equity (see Cawelti, 2001; McAdams, 2000; Skrla, Scheurich, & Johnson, 2000; Skrla & Scheurich, 2001). Skrla and Scheurich (2001) argue that such examples are found more often in states with well-established, stable accountability systems with equity-oriented components, such as North Carolina and Texas, and that state accountability systems played a key role by pushing for success. Nevertheless, it is argued that successful schools in Texas tend to be outliers and that their success is not easily transferable to many other typical schools under similar circumstances (Valencia et al., 2004). As the researchers whose studies showed the positive impact of accountability on equity often acknowledged, lower class sizes and increased, more equitable funding in Texas have created a context in which the accountability system could increase equity (Grissmer et al., 2000; Skrla et al., 2004).

On the other hand, accountability policy may widen achievement gaps by rewarding advantaged, high-performing students and their schools and punishing disadvantaged ones. By raising performance standards and stakes without assuring equity in key school inputs, this policy could have had the effect of making schools focus on advantaged high-performing students who were more likely to meet the standards.[4] Ceci and Papierno (2005) argue that universalized educational interventions often have the unintended consequences of widening pre-existing achievement gaps as more advantaged groups may benefit more from the interventions than their disadvantaged counterparts. Inequity may be also exacerbated when educationally irrelevant factors such as race and socioeconomic status filter institutional support for schooling. In brief, education is subject to the phenomenon of so-called Matthew effects: the rich gets richer, and the poor gets poorer.

Previous studies on the impact of high-stakes testing and accountability policies showed the effects of policy on academic motivation and behaviors, including changes in students' course taking (Shiller & Mueller,

2003), student motivation (Roderick & Engel, 2001), and teacher motivation (Kelley, Heneman, & Milanowski, 2000). Some states or school districts' larger achievement gains in the 1990s were attributed to more rigorous testing and stronger accountability policy (Bishop, Mane, Bishop, & Moriarty, 2001; Carnoy & Loeb, 2002; Clotfelter & Ladd, 1996; Grissmer & Flagnan, 1998; Raymond & Hanushek, 2003). The cost of test-based accountability was deemed so small that it held out the hope of greater cost-effectiveness (Hoxby, 2002).

However, some studies challenge simple, rationalistic approaches to performance-driven accountability policy and identify contingencies for policy success. Some show that the effects of high-stakes testing and accountability policy on student achievement are largely indeterminate or mixed (Amrein & Berliner, 2002; Jacob, 2001; Lee, 1998a). Some studies suggest that externally set standards and tests may serve as extrinsic motivations for academic press, but that their ultimate effects on academic performance depend on school capacity and social support (Lee & Smith, 1999; Newmann, King, & Rigdon, 1997). Recent work on the impact of high-stakes testing in Chicago suggests that the additional resources provided to at-risk students, such as reduced class sizes, after-school tutoring, and summer school programs, enhances achievement gains (Roderick, Bryk, Jacob, Easton, & Allensworth, 1999).

TENSION BETWEEN ACADEMIC EXCELLENCE AND EQUITY

Despite the policy imperative of achieving both academic excellence and equity simultaneously, there are tensions between the two goals (Gardner, 1984; Green, 1982; Noddings, 1992). A system of education would fall short of excellence if it fell short of equity, that is, if a substantial number of students were unjustly denied access to educational opportunities they wanted and from which they could profit. The caution against pursuing academic excellence at the cost of equity is also found in *A Nation at Risk* (NCEE, 1983):

> We do not believe that a public commitment to excellence and educational reform must be made at the expense of a strong public commitment to the equitable treatment of our diverse population. The twin goals of equity and high-quality schooling have profound and practical meaning for our economy and society, and we cannot permit one to yield to the other in principle or in practice.

How well did the nation accomplish both academic excellence and equity at the same time? A glimpse at the past trends of student achievement on long-term trend NAEP shows remarkable progress on the equity front without commensurable success on the excellence front. Overall, student achievement improved to a small or moderate extent during the last three decades: 1971–2004 in reading and 1973–2004 in mathematics (see Figures 3 and 4). Accumulating annual gains over the entire NAEP testing period of 33 years, the average reading achievement improved by about 10 percent of one standard deviation (.003 SD per year times 33 = .1), whereas the average math achievement improved by about 50 percent of one standard deviation (.015 SD per year times 33 = .50).[5] Clearly, there was much greater academic improvement in math than in reading. This trend may be interpreted as evidence in support of school improvement since reading achievement tends to be more highly influenced by children's family background and prior experiences than does math achievement (Murnane, 1975). Math achievement may be more sensitive to the effects of school reform than reading. However, there are no clear indications that the average achievement improvement is related to educational reform policies. As shown by the linear achievement trend lines based on fitting time-series regression analysis, both national reading and math performance trajectories did not change significantly after key national educational events that influenced educational accountability policies: a Nation at Risk of 1983, Goals 2000 and IASA of 1994, and NCLB of 2001 (marked by reference lines on the horizontal axis of Figures 2 and 3).

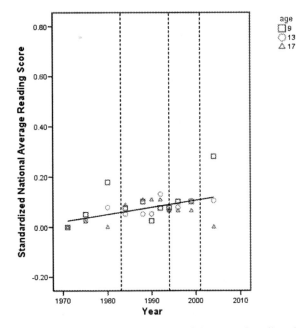

Figure 2.   NAEP Long-term Trends in National Average Reading Scores (in standard deviation units).

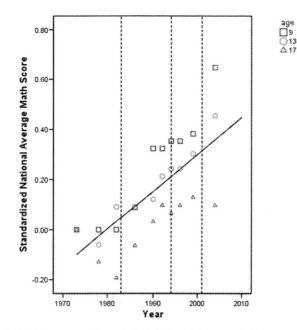

Figure 3.   NAEP Long-term Trends in National Average Math Scores (in standard deviation units).

The above trends of reading and math achievement came from the long-term trend NAEP that has more focus on basic skills: the computational focus gives information on how students are performing on traditional procedural skills and most questions are completed in multiple-choice format without use of a calculator. A question may be raised: Is the trend of flat reading vs. growing math achievement also evident on main NAEP which reflects more recent math standards and thus can be more consistent with current teaching and learning practices? The answer is yes. But it is important to note that main NAEP has shown more improvement than long-term trend NAEP during the 1990s (see Loveless, 2006).[6] Part II of this book relies on the main NAEP results to take a closer look at recent reading and math achievement trends, particularly in relation to NCLB.

At the same time, the long-term NAEP trend of racial achievement gap shows a significant narrowing of the Black–White and Hispanic–White test score gaps in reading and mathematics during the last three decades. The Black–White test score gaps fell by 0.4 in standard deviation units in reading and mathematics over the 1971/1973–1990 period (see Figure 4 and Figure 5). While the Hispanic–White gap followed a similar pattern, the Hispanic–White achievement gaps were relatively smaller than the Black–White gaps and changed to a lesser extent throughout the period.

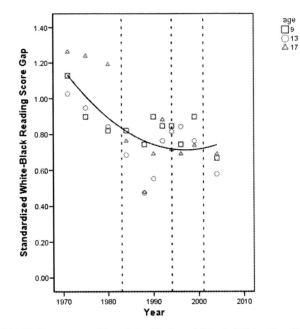

Figure 4.   NAEP Long-term Trends in National Black–White Reading Score Gaps (in standard deviation units).

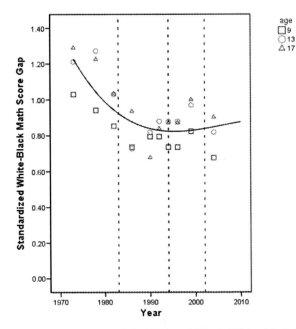

Figure 5.   NAEP Long-term Trends in National Black–White Math Score Gaps (in standard deviation units).

The reduction of racial achievement gaps through the 1970s and 1980s signified great progress in equity. However, there were setbacks in national progress toward equity during the last decade when racial achievement gaps stabilized or widened (Lee, 2002). Currently, the overall Black–White and Hispanic–White mathematics achievement gaps remain substantially large, with the ranges of those gaps falling between .7 and 1 in standard deviation units.[7]

Although the main NAEP assessment results are not directly comparable to the long-term trend NAEP because of their differences in student samples as well as test content/format, both assessment results demonstrate that the racial achievement gaps in mathematics increased from 1990 to 2000: estimated increases in the size of the gap from the main NAEP appear to be slightly larger than estimates from the long-term NAEP (see Lee, 2004c). Part II of this book takes an in-depth look into the achievement gap trends based on the main NAEP results.

There were modestly inverse relationships between the national average achievement and racial achievement gaps in reading and math over the last three decades. For example, the correlation between average math score and White–Black gap is significantly negative ($r = -.47$, $p < .01$). This implies that the national average achievement of all students has improved to some extent while the gaps between racial groups narrowed and that the narrowing of the gaps was not accomplished at the cost of lowering White students' achievement. It suggests that academic excellence and equity can be pursued simultaneously despite tensions between the two goals. However, it needs to be noted that Black–White gaps in achievement decreased during the 1970s–1980s when the emphasis was on minimum competency (basic skills), but increased during the 1990s, when the emphasis shifted to proficiency (higher-order skills) (Lee, 2002). This raises the question as to whether these patterns are caused by reform-oriented instruction, differential access to such instruction, or other confounding variables (Lubienski, 2006).

Why did racial and socioeconomic achievement gaps narrow substantially in the 1970s? During the 1970s, education and social policies worked to narrow the achievement gap by guaranteeing a minimally adequate level of achievement for minorities through compensatory education, minimum competency testing, school desegregation, equalization of school funding, the War on Poverty, and affirmative action. Figure 6 illustrates this situation where the interventions targeting low-achieving students (mostly low-income minority students) help them meet a minimally adequate level of performance (basic skills). Murnane and Levy (1996) point out that 17-year-olds should score 300 or more on the NAEP reading and mathematics tests in order to meet the New Basic Skills, the minimum skills people now need to get a middle-class job. If we accept level 300 as the minimally adequate level of achievement for high school graduates, Black and Hispanic

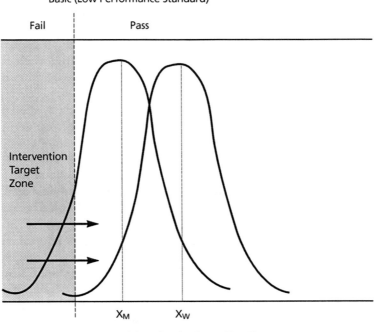

Figure 6.   Hypothetical Distributions of White vs. Minority Academic Achievement and Pass/Fail under Test-driven Accountability Intervention in the 1970s and 1980s (Minimum Competency Test for Low-Achieving Students as Target).

students did make significant progress toward that goal over the last two decades. Nevertheless, the progress almost stalled during the 1990s, and the gap of Blacks and Hispanics in basic knowledge and skills still remains very large. As of 1999, 27% of Black and 38% of Hispanic 17-year-olds performed at or above level 300 in mathematics. The corresponding figure for their White peers was 70%. This educational intervention acted in conjunction with social policies by combining a performance-guarantee approach (minimum competency testing for promotion and graduation) with an input-guarantee approach.

As the focus of education policy has shifted from equity to excellence during the last two decades, there is a potential tension between academic excellence and equity (Bracey, 2002; O'Day & Smith, 1993). Figure 7 illustrates this situation where the target of interventions shifted to all students, including the higher-achieving advantaged White students, by setting a higher performance standard (proficiency). In the 1990s, racial achievement gaps stopped narrowing or began to widen, signaling setbacks in the progress the nation made toward educational equity (Lee, 2002).[8]

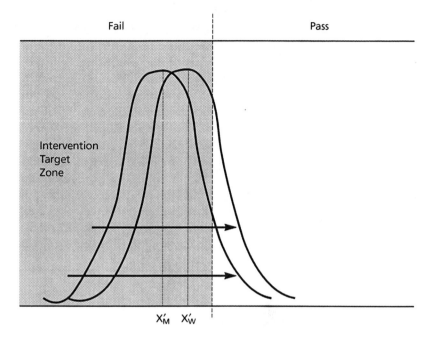

White-Minority Gap = $X'_W - X'_M$

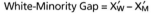

Figure 7.   Hypothetical Distributions of White vs. Minority Achievement and Pass/Fail under Test-driven Accountability Intervention in the 1990s and 2000s (Proficiency Test for both Low-achieving and High-Achieving Students as Target).

INTERSTATE VARIATIONS IN ACADEMIC EXCELLENCE AND EQUITY

The tension between academic excellence and equity is observed at the state level as well. States were not effective in addressing educational inequalities and achievement gaps in the 1990s (Barton, 2002; Braun, Wang, Jenkins, Weinbaum, 2006; Lee & Wong, 2004). The gaps remain substantial as of 2005. For example, the 2005 NAEP report not only shows that the percentage of Black and Hispanic students performing at or above the Proficient level in mathematics is much lower than that of their White peers (47% for Whites vs. 13% for Blacks and 19% for Hispanics at grade 4; 39% for Whites vs. 9% for Blacks and 13% for Hispanics at grade 8), but it also shows that a large majority of Black students fail to meet the proficiency standard. Simply reducing disparities in test scores is not sufficient without also improving the percentage of low-achieving students and disadvantaged minority groups that perform at or above the NAEP proficiency level. However, there remain controversies about the validity of the NAEP proficiency level due to severe discrepancies between NAEP and states' own assessment results (see Fuller, Gesicki, Kang & Wright, 2006; Klein, Hamilton, McCaffrey, & Stecher, 2000; Koretz & Barron, 1998; Lee, in press; Linn, Baker, & Betebenner, 2002; Loveless, 2006).

Figures 9 and 10 show NAEP 2003 8th grade math results for the nation and states in light of the relationship between average math achievement and achievement gaps. The horizontal axis shows the average math test score for all students, whereas the vertical axis shows the average test score gap between white and black students (Figure 8) and between non-poor and poor students (Figure 9). We find enormous interstate variation in not only the average achievement but also in the size of achievement gaps. However, there are no systematic relationships between the average achievement and achievement gaps. Higher performing states do not differ significantly from lower performing states in the size of White–Black

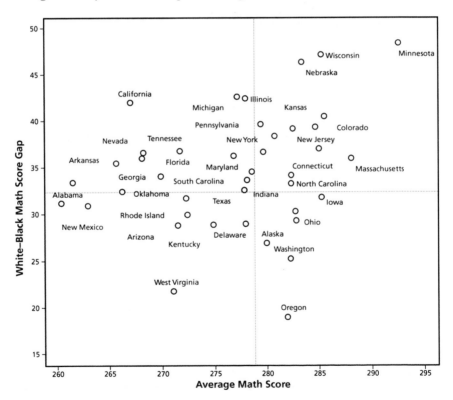

Figure 8.   Plot of 2003 NAEP state 8th grade math White–Black achievement gap vs. average achievement.

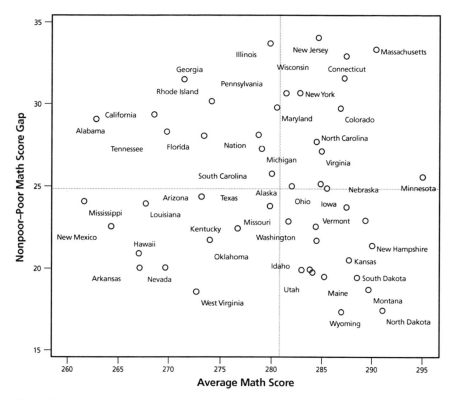

Figure 9.   Plot of 2003 NAEP state 8th grade math Nonpoor–Poor achievement gap vs. average achievement.

gap ($r = .27$). At the same time, higher-performing states have neither larger nor smaller achievement gaps between the socially advantaged and disadvantaged ($r = -.04$). This indicates that there are very few states that accomplish both academic excellence and equity. On the other hand, the correlation between White–Black achievement gap and non-poor vs. poor achievement gap is moderately positive ($r = .51$), which means that racial and social achievement gaps may share some common causes.

Given the above patterns of student outcomes, we may classify states into four types, depending on the level of average achievement and the level of racial/social achievement gaps (see Figure 10). For example, Connecticut, California, Kentucky, and Maine, exemplify each cell of this two-way classification table. According to the NAEP 2003 8th grade math results, Kentucky and California were examples of relatively low-achieving states (weak for excellence), whereas Connecticut and Maine were examples of high-performing states relative to the national average (strong for excellence). At the same time, Connecticut and California were examples of relatively

		Equity (Achievement gaps)	
		Strong (Small gap)	Weak (Large gap)
Excellence (Average Achievement)	Strong (High average)	High on Both Excellence and Equity (e.g., Maine)	High on Excellence and Low on Equity (e.g., Connecticut)
	Weak (Low average)	Low on Excellence and High on Equity (e.g., Kentucky)	Low on Both Excellence and Equity (e.g., California)

Figure 10.   Classification of states by the level of average academic achievement and the size of achievement gaps (racial and socioeconomic gaps).

large-gap states (weak for equity), while Kentucky and Maine were examples of relatively small-gap states compared with the national norm (strong for equity).

The above variations among the four states can be accounted for partly by their differences in demographic compositions and schooling conditions (Lee, 2007). Do state accountability policies account for student outcomes above and beyond demographic and schooling factors? While all of the four states set challenging performance standards in the 1990s, these states' choices of policy approaches to reaching the standards differed. Kentucky and California, which were performing much below the national average at the time of standards-setting, saw greater needs for improvement and became more active in test-driven accountability. States that adopted accountability polices before NCLB are called "first-generation" accountability states and include Kentucky, Maryland, North Carolina, California, Florida, New York, and Texas (Mintrop & Trujillo, 2005). In contrast, Connecticut and Maine, which were performing much above the national average, hardly felt a crisis and did not actively join the bandwagon of high-stakes testing. States that never initiated statewide accountability reform before NCLB are called "second-generation" accountability states for the sake of distinction, whether they embraced NCLB or not.[9]

CALL FOR SCIENTIFIC TRIALS OF TEST-DRIVEN EDUCATIONAL ACCOUNTABILITY POLICIES

The overview of issues related to accountability policy, research and practice calls for scientific trials. In the past, educational research failed to well inform educational policy and practice due to its often politicized, fragmented, and impractical work (Kaestle, 1993). While the current educational policy talk under NCLB pushes for more scientifically based research and randomized experiments in particular, it has generated new controversies as to what constitutes scientific research and evidence-based policy (NRC, 2002; Slavin, 2002). However, the term "scientific" or "evidence-based" should not be simply dismissed as politically loaded to discourage neutral applications. In this book, I use the term "scientific" in its common sense in order to emphasize the need for rigorous, empirical and falsifiable research to better inform and evaluate educational policy.[10]

Part I of this book addresses concerns about scientific, institutional, and technical threats to the validity of current test-driven educational accountability systems in the nation and states. Scientific threats to a test-driven educational accountability system arise when the legitimacy of policy is threatened by its reliance on limited and possibly biased source of research evidence. Institutional threats arise when top-down policy mandates for achieving unrealistically high performance standards meet school realities in which different professional values, limited instructional capacity and resources undermine the fidelity of policy implementation. Technical threats to an accountability system arise when high-stakes testing faces measurement challenges by which desirable psychometric properties (validity, reliability, and fairness) of testing and accountability measures are lacking and questionable. The book offers new insights into the design and evaluation of educational accountability systems by assessing these threats and discussing possible remedies that help counteract the threats.

Part II of this book examines the achievement gap trends based on NAEP and state assessments before and after NCLB in order to shed light on controversies about the impact of test-driven educational accountability from both academic excellence and equity perspectives. It examines whether the nation and states that attempted to hold schools, teachers, and/or students accountable for academic performance (a performance-driven approach) accomplished that goal, with or without fulfillment of their own responsibility to increase the availability of adequate resources overall and equalize the allocation of resources (an input-driven approach). More specifically, did strong performance-driven-accountability states provide support for school resources and address racial and socio-economic disparities in access to resources? And were those strong accountability states, with or without such support, able to improve the achievement of disadvantaged minority students and narrow the achievement gaps? The time frame for these analyses is the 1990s and early 2000s, when federal and state accountability policy initiatives may have had impact on student outcomes. In the midst of a keen policy debate about the impact of high-stakes testing and accountability initiatives on equity, this study has implications for contemporary national and state policy efforts, as mandated by the NCLB, to close the achievement gap.

Part III of this book wraps up the policy debate with summary of key findings and policy recommendations. Keeping track of national/state education policies and student achievement outcomes should contribute to our understanding of educational policy impact. The research in this book will inform us about whether changes in student achievement gaps are coincidental or systematically related to educational policy shifts. In the midst of keen debate on test-driven external accountability policies under NCLB, the study will help us become more aware of the assumptions that may have been part of policy shifts and their potential consequences for equity. The study is expected to contribute to the field of educational policy studies by proposing and testing a model for examining the relationship between changes in national/state policies and student outcomes.

NOTES

1. In 2005, the State of Connecticut sued the U.S. Department of Education over insufficient funding and support from the federal government to help the state meet the testing provisions of NCLB (*Connecticut v. Spellings*).

2. The pure form of this arrangement was referred to as a tight-loose-tight governance structure, in which the central authority *tightly* specifies schools' missions and outcome standards, *loosely* allows schools to use whatever methods they choose to achieve those standards, and then *tightly* holds schools accountable for results.

3. While many studies examined the average policy effect for all students, only a few (e.g., Carnoy & Loeb, 2002; Hanushek & Raymond, 2004; Lee & Wong, 2004) disaggregated the results by racial subgroups and explored potential accountability policy effects on racial achievement gaps. For a recent comprehensive review of the literature on accountability policy impact, see Harris and Herrington (2006) and Lee (2006a).

4. Major concerns are that the state's emphasis on its "goal" overlooks the progress made by lower-performing students who meet or exceed the minimum competency level and has a chilling effect on teachers who have moved a significant number of students above that basic level.

5. The means and standard deviations of NAEP scores vary among age levels. In order to compute standardized gain scores that are comparable among age groups in each subject, national average NAEP scale score in each year was subtracted from its baseline year (1971 for reading and 1973 for math) average score and then the difference score was divided by within-age standard deviation of student scores: $M = 208$, $SD = 40$ for reading age 9; $M = 255$, $SD = 37$ for reading age 13; $M = 285$, $SD = 42$ for reading age 17; $M = 219$, $SD = 34$ for math age 9; $M = 266$, $SD = 33$ for math age 13; $M = 304$, $SD = 31$ for math age 17.

6. NAEP long-term trend assessments are designed to give information on the changes in the basic achievement of America's youth. They have measured

student achievement at ages 9, 13, and 17 since the early 1970s. This differs from main NAEP that is relatively new and designed to give the most up-to-date and standards-based student achievement information based on new curriculum. They have measured student achievement at grades 4, 8, and 12 since 1990. See the NAEP homepage for more information on each of the assessment at http://www.nces.ed.gov/nationsreportcard/.

7.   Interpretation of the achievement gap on NAEP can be facilitated by using some sort of effect size metrics. One way to think about the size of the achievement gap is to consider how large the gap is relative to the standard deviation of NAEP scores. One standard deviation of the NAEP scores is in an about 30–40 point range. Another way to think about the size of the achievement gap is to consider how large the gap is relative to the average amount of gain score per grade on the NAEP scale. The yearly learning gain on the NAEP scale is about 10 points. Therefore, the racial achievement gap of one standard deviation amounts to 3–4 years of learning gap.

8.   For diverse perspectives on the issue of closing the achievement gap, see Jencks and Phillips (1998), Peterson (2006), and Rothstein (2004).

9.   The four states not only varied in performance-driven accountability policies but also in input-regulation policies such as course-taking requirement for high school graduation and teacher certification. Among the first-generation accountability states, Kentucky was strong and Maryland was weak in input regulations. Among the second-generation states, Connecticut was strong and Maine was weak in input regulations.

10.   Specifically, scientific research requires that researchers (1) put hypotheses about a policy to a rigorous test to see if they hold up with valid and reliable data and (2) make all aspects of the investigation public and described in sufficient detail that the study can be repeated and falsified by any who question the results.

PART I

POLICY, RESEARCH AND PRACTICE OF TEST-DRIVEN EXTERNAL ACCOUNTABILITY

CHAPTER 1

EDUCATIONAL POLICY LABORATORY

Scientific Trials of Accountability

THE EBB AND FLOW OF DISCOURSE ABOUT ACCOUNTABILITY, EXCELLENCE AND EQUITY ISSUES

There were several major environmental changes that influenced educational reform movement during the past two decades. State education reform of the past two decades is unique in terms of the scope and momentum of the movement. The reform agenda has been sustained longer than previous efforts. The sustaining source of reform is also different: a major source of reform comes from outside the school system. There is greater public attention and a wider coalition of reform actors than often has been the case in the past (Underwood, 1989). *A Nation at Risk* created a crisis atmosphere, connecting U.S. economic decline with educational performance and suggesting that educational upgrading would lead to economic revitalization (National Commission on Excellence in Education, 1983). Conservative Republican control, modernization of state governments, and economic recovery contributed to the resurgence of the states' role in American federalism, particularly in the provision of new infrastructure for local development (Nathan, 1990). Further, the development of information technology facilitated faster policy diffusion across the nation by allowing state and local policy actors to access information on school reform via

The Testing Gap, pages 27–37
Copyright © 2007 by Information Age Publishing
All rights of reproduction in any form reserved.

an electronic network or forum. More clear-cut, low-cost, and easy-to-implement school reform package including high-stakes testing for accountability have gained popularity.

A quick review of past educational studies and media reports gives a glimpse into the fads or trends of public discourse about the issues of accountability, excellence and equity under standards-based education reform. For the sake of illustration, I chose the Educational Resources Information Center (ERIC) database and Education Week (EW) archives. Using ERIC and EW databases, doing key word searches for a combination of terms "standards and accountability", "standards and excellence" "standards and equity" produce very similar trends in both research and media reports over the past two decades (see Figure 1.1 and Figure 1.2). The coincidence of trends in research and media reports reflect common social forces, policy issues or fads that influenced both communities. It is not clear which shaped which (policy shaped research or vice versa).

While the research and media coverage of accountability was pretty stable during the 1980s, there was a sudden dramatic increase in the number of research and media reports on the topic in the early 1990s. What was the reason for this surge of accountability as a buzzword across the nation and states? When was the tipping point that test-driven or performance-driven

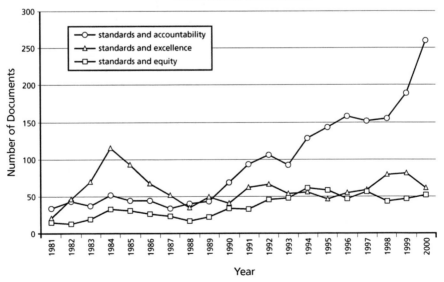

Figure 1.1.   The trend of educational research on standards-based education policy topics based on 1981–2000 ERIC database searches with key words "standards" in tandem with "accountability," "excellence," and "equity."

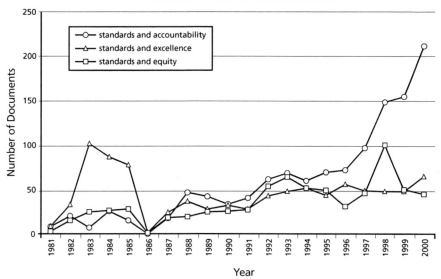

Figure 1.2.   The trend of educational media on standards-based education policy topics based on 1981–2000 *Education Week* database searches with key words "standards" in tandem with "accountability," "excellence," and "equity."

accountability issues dominate educational policy discourse and shape educational research agenda? One significant accountability milestone took place in 1989 at the National Education Summit of state governors to establish education goals for 2000 (Walberg, 2003). This Goals 2000 program was enacted into law in 1994, pushing for national standards and assessments (Ravitch, 1995). At the same time, the Improving America's Schools Act of 1994 (IASA), the law that reauthorizes the Elementary and Secondary Education Act of 1965 (ESEA), reinforced the performance-based school accountability movement. Once the accountability movement got momentum, the volume of media attention and research investigation quickly doubled, tripled and quadrupled over the last decade. This shift in the trend coincides with the timing of national education goals. The coverage of excellence had a temporary peak in the early 1980s, possibly due to the 1983 *A Nation at Risk* report, but then it leveled off. In contrast, the coverage of equity has maintained a low profile throughout the past two decades.

Debates on high-stakes testing under NCLB of 2001 has drawn much media attention. For instance, PBS Frontline's special coverage of NCLB and high-stakes testing issues, "Testing Our Schools" (http://www.pbs.org/wgbh/pages/frontline/shows/schools/), posed the key question: "Will more testing and tougher accountability change public education for the better?" At one end of the debate, champions of high-stakes testing point out its overwhelming benefits (see Bishop, 2001; Hanushek & Raymond, 2004; Phelps, 2005). At the other extreme, critics argue for revamping a test-driven external school accountability system under NCLB (see Elmore, 2002; Sirotnik, 2004; Sunderman, Kim, & Orfield, 2005). However, the reasons cited for either approval or disapproval are not always grounded in research. As Connecticut filed a lawsuit challenging NCLB as unfunded mandates, the state Commissioner of Education Betty J. Sternberg said at the press conference: "There is no research base that tells us that additional testing of this type will yield better results" (August 22, 2005).

While there has been a strong call for evidence-based education policy, the validation of policies requires that they stand up to rigorous scientific scrutiny (NRC, 2002; Slavin, 2002). Currently there are independent, bipartisan efforts underway to improve NCLB, such as the Commission on No Child Left Behind Act, which plans to report to Congress and the Administration with recommendations for changes based on hearings and research. Are the current federal and state governments' test-driven external accountability policies scientifically valid and legitimate? Is there strong evidence that NCLB works for improving academic excellence and equity? As prior research has produced mixed findings and researchers tend to polarize between the extremes, there is a growing need for synthesis of the research findings from balanced and objective perspectives.

MAPPING OUT INTERSTATE EDUCATION REFORM AND ACCOUNTABILITY POLICIES

The 1980s and 1990s have been characterized as the decade of state education reform (Fuhrman, 1988; Murphy, 1990). The states increased course credit requirements for graduation, raised standards for teacher preparation, mandated teacher tests for certification, set higher levels for teacher pay, developed state curriculum frameworks or guides, and established new statewide student assessments (Blank & Dalkilic, 1992). Although most states have gradually built up greater authority and responsibility over their educational systems, the substance and structure of reform varies widely across the country (Mitchell, Roysdon, Wirt, & Marshall, 1990).

School accountability policies need to be understood in light of such standards-based, systemic education reform efforts. The development of curriculum standards, curriculum-assessment alignment, teacher certification standards, and professional development efforts constitute a broader context of standards-based (content-driven) education reform in which accountability policies are embedded. Such measures of standards-based education reform were constructed earlier by Lee (1997) and by Swanson

and Stevenson (2002). Many kinds of reform elements have been combined under a single statute in several states. Moreover, the well-publicized
context of school reform efforts in other states and a pervasive sense of
raising educational standards were also underlying factors that cut across
issues and time. These factors allowed researchers to systematically examine state education policymaking through the Rasch measurement
method, an application of item response theory to policy analysis. It was
found that most of the leading states in the first-wave education reform are
concentrated in the South with relatively low socioeconomic status and low
educational attainment. In a similar vein, many academically lower-performing states were more active in standards-based education reform.
These earlier standards-based (input-driven or content-driven) reform policy measures had moderate correlations with subsequent performance-
driven accountability policy measures.

Lee and Wong (2004) measured state accountability policies with survey
data collected in the mid-to-late 1990s from three sources: (a) 1995–1996
data from the North Central Regional Education Laboratory (NCREL) and
the Council of Chief State School Officers (CCSSO) (NCREL/CCSSO,
1996); (b) 1999 data from the Quality Counts (QC) report ("Quality Counts
'99," 1999); and (c) 1999–2000 data from the Consortium for Policy
Research in Education (CPRE) report (Goertz & Duffy, 2001). This factor
analysis combined the three sources of survey data and classified the 50
states into three groups: those with strong accountability systems (12 states
in the top quartile), those with moderate accountability systems (25 states in
the middle half), and those with weak accountability systems (13 states in the
bottom quartile). States with strong accountability systems included Alabama,
Florida, Illinois, Indiana, Kentucky, Louisiana, Maryland, New Jersey, New
Mexico, New York, North Carolina, and Texas. In contrast, states with weak
accountability systems included: Alaska, Arkansas, Colorado, Delaware,
Idaho, Iowa, Maine, Massachusetts, Montana, Nebraska, New Hampshire,
North Dakota, and Wyoming (see Appendix A).

Since this classification and labeling of "strong" and "weak" accountability states was created in a purely relative sense, with reference to the distri
bution of actual state policy measures, a more meaningful comparison of
the two groups of states would need a substantive definition of strong
accountability and descriptions of actual adopted policies. It is possible
that even the strongest accountability system in the distribution might be
fairly weak when we consider what the hypothetical ends of an accountability continuum might be. Strong accountability systems are often defined as
those in which states have in place and can use all of the following policy
instruments: report cards and ratings of schools, rewards for successful
schools, and reconstitution or major alteration of failing schools (see Finn
& Kanstoroom, 2001; Walberg, 2003). What is missing in this definition of

strong accountability is adequate assistance and support to schools—the key component of shared responsibility. Our norm-referenced classification of strong and weak accountability turns out to be largely consistent with this sort of criterion-referenced classification by Finn and Kanstoroom (2001). States that have different classifications are Louisiana and New Jersey (classified as weak accountability by Finn & Kanstoroom). According to Finn and Kanstoroom (2001), some strong accountability states have shaky foundations or inferior academic standards. The Finn-Kanstoroom criteria (clear, measurable, comprehensive, and rigorous) for assessing the quality of curriculum standards may be debatable, but their relevance to assessing the impact of accountability on achievement outcomes remains to be examined.

Figure 1.3 shows the percentages of states in strong-versus-weak accountability categories that had adopted selected accountability policies as of 1999. Although most weak accountability states also had state assessment, and some even had report cards for schools, none of them provided direct incentives to schools in the form of performance ratings, rewards, assistance, and sanctions. In contrast, most strong accountability states turned out to have these key elements of accountability policy in place. Some states in the top quartile of our accountability scale did not adopt all major policies. If strong accountability states are expected to have all of these in place to maximize policy effects, then only five states would meet that expectation.

Given natural variations among the 50 states in educational policies and student outcomes, states provide a laboratory for investigating how school reform policies work. However, these social experiments were not carefully designed for evaluation. As with most other policies, test-driven external

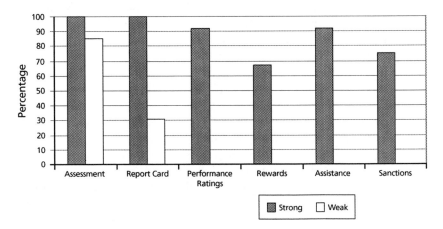

Figure 1.3.   Percentages of strong accountability states and weak accountability states that adopted various school accountability policies.

accountability policies were nonrandomized, uncontrolled trials that preclude systematic evaluations. Strong accountability states tend to be different from weak accountability states in terms of their demographic composition of student population, particularly racial and socioeconomic characteristics that might have resulted in different outcomes. Any causal inferences drawn from interstate comparisons of policy outcomes are not warranted because of the possibility of extraneous variables that may confound our results. Prior to their policy adoption, strong accountability states tended to have poorer student outcomes. The initially lower achievement level of strong accountability states may be explained by the fact that they had larger minority populations and relatively unfavorable social and family conditions for children's education (e.g., lower median household income and lower educational attainment among the total population). Despite these interstate variations in social and educational context, NCLB has taken a "one size fits all" approach by attempting to spread one model of test-driven accountability across the nation, including those weak accountability states.

THE JURY IS STILL OUT: SINK OR SWIM?

There is a public perception that state education accountability policy has replaced "inputs" with "outcomes" across the nation in the last two decades. According to an educational media report, states have moved from "inputs" to "outcomes" in an effort to regulate schools, concluding that more traditional practices of regulating school inputs have failed (Education Week, March 13, 1993). In other words, the states were believed to have given greater autonomy to schools in return for results on academic performance. This perceived policy shift, however, oversimplifies the nature and extent of changes that resulted from state education reform during the last two decades and obscures variations among the 50 states. Many states sought mainly to expand or improve educational inputs (e.g., longer school day, advanced courses, better teachers) during the period following the publication of A Nation at Risk in 1983. Later, following the release of National Education Goals in 1990, states attempted to develop more challenging performance standards and to hold schools accountable for meeting those standards. The number of states that used student assessment results for accountability purposes increased. At the same time, states maintained or strengthened policies that regulated educational inputs. Thus, contrary to the conventional knowledge of a state policy shift, it appears that policies to regulate outcomes were added to policies that regulate inputs, rather than replaced them.

Although accountability policies appear to have shifted from an input-guarantee approach to a performance-guarantee approach, their function has been largely "regulatory" rather than "supportive," relying more on mandates and sanctions than on capacity building and rewards. Indeed, the relationship between state activism in accountability policy and support for school resources is very tenuous, implying that state activism in test-driven external accountability was not accompanied by state support for school resources (see Lee & Wong, 2004). Accountability and systemic reform also tend to define support somewhat narrowly, focusing on technical assistance and professional development for curriculum and instruction. Professional development and technical assistance can have greater effects when the resources and environment, including favorable class size and qualified teachers, are already adequate. The central question is how all schools are provided with educational resources and technical assistance to ensure that they are able to help their students meet the high standards.

According to *Quality Counts 2001* report, 49 states had statewide academic standards, 50 states had statewide testing and 27 states held schools accountable for results. Among those 27, only 7 states provided extra funding for all low-performing schools. Of the 18 states that required high school exit examinations at that time, only 9 states were found to help subsidize remediation for failing students. Of the 42 states that provided some money for professional development, only 24 earmarked professional development funds specifically for every local school or district. This also implies that the accountability movement was not reciprocal. In other words, while state legislatures and state education agencies attempted to hold schools, teachers and students accountable for performance outcomes, state legislators and state education agencies themselves were not held accountable for providing support and assistance to those target schools, teachers and students.

By January 2002, when NCLB took effect, only about one-third of states had fully met the standards and assessment requirements for NCLB's predecessor, the IASA (Erpenbarch, Forte-Fast, & Potts, 2003). NCLB has tightened enforcement of the law since many states did not faithfully implement the IASA policy. Nevertheless, recent studies of NCLB policy implementation by the American Institutes for Research (AIR) show variability among states and districts in their school support mechanism (AIR, 2006). 37 states used support teams and 29 of them included individual professionals to assist schools identified as needing improvement. States tended to provide more technical assistance rather than sanctions and few schools were asked for restructuring. The AIR study also raises questions about the timeliness and utility of this identification. Only 31 states provided preliminary results before Sep, 2004 but 20 did not. This suggests that schools cannot plan for improvement and seek assistance even after a new school year has begun. This is analogous to closing the barn door after a horse is stolen. School principals reported that they needed assistance in diverse areas including professional development, curriculum and instruction, and test-taking strategies. The AIR study also reveals that school improvement efforts included increased time for reading and/or math, and after-school tutoring. Under NCLB, there are options for school transfer and supplementary education service (SES). However, school choice is constrained by an absence of non-identified schools in a district. Further, because of the state's late notification of school status, most districts did not notify parents of choice options before school started. SES can be helpful but most states are in the early stage of monitoring and evaluating service providers (most private and some district/school-based).

Under these circumstances, is NCLB's AYP target (100% Proficient) attainable by 2014? It was estimated that up to 80 percent of schools in some states could be targeted as needing improvement or corrective action in the first few years under NCLB (Marion et al., 2002; Olson, 2002, April 18; Lee, 2004b). If the AYP target is unrealistically high and dooms schools, particularly ones with predominantly disadvantaged minority students, to failure, it may lead to unintended negative consequences. States may try gaming with the system to dodge federal sanctions, procrastination of the AYP goal schedule to delay the process, excluding students and/or lowering the target standard to inflate test results. An analysis by the Associated Press found that the test scores of nearly 2 million students, mostly minorities, were not being counted for subgroup performance and many schools were escaping accountability for the progress of racial and ethnic subgroups as a result of exclusion practices (Davis, 2006). The procrastination of policy implementation, goal reduction, exclusion of students from test reporting, and score inflation all threaten the validity of accountability policy.

No matter what tactics that the states may use in response to the federal mandate, real implementation problems may still occur down at the school and classroom levels. Some studies pointed out the lack of school capacity and resources to meet such a high performance target. Despite the expectations of shared responsibility or symmetric accountability for academic improvement, concerns about an exclusive focus on educators and/or students while ignoring other responsible parties including policymakers have been raised (Linn, 2003; Porter & Chester, 2002). Studies show that assessment and accountability policies imposed changes in schools with little to no support over the long haul and that this unfunded mandate has created problems. New state assessment in Arizona came without support for teacher training and ceding responsibility to districts produced disparities in staff development (Smith, Heinecke, & Noble, 1999). The same problem was also observed in other countries where additional funding to support similar reforms in schools was limited and little attention was given to the reallocation of resources (Levin, 2001).

STANDARDIZED TESTING FOR SCHOOL ACCOUNTABILITY: BOOST OR BUST?

What are the major technical threats to the validity of accountability policy? How valid, reliable and fair are the test measures that are the basis of decisions for school accountability? How do those decisions (or simply the threat of sanctions) have an impact on teaching and learning in schools?

The current accountability policy in the U.S. is unique in that it calls upon measurement and statistical knowledge base. Measurement issues concern the validity, reliability, fairness and utility of test measures. For example, Murray (2006) dismisses the NCLB measures as uninformative and deceptive. Even when we have appropriate, accurate, fair and useful measures in place, it remains challenging to make valid causal attribution of the measured outcomes to school effects because there are likely to be so many unmeasured variables (e.g., home and community effects) that may confound the results and proper statistical control for such external influences is not readily done. Popham (2004) likens the problem to "measuring temperature with a tablespoon" and also calls for "assessment literacy education campaign."

NCLB's high-stakes testing policy gives public schools unprecedented pressure for academic improvement with consequences attached to statewide test results. Some critical measurement and statistical problems foreshadow technical challenges that lie ahead of NCLB's AYP: first, is the AYP measure consistent and accurate? If the AYP measure changes too much by chance, it will lose validity. Second, is the AYP formula unbiased and fair? If the AYP formula treats unequal schools equally, it will render the outcomes inequitable and lessen validity. Third, is the AYP decision-making comprehensive and holistic? There are possible hazards of evaluating school performance based on a single measure.

Increasing threats to the validity of test-driven school accountability system may endanger nationwide systemic efforts to advance the goal of educational excellence and equity for all students. The seriousness of some threats may have been inflated, while that of other threats may have been underestimated. Scrutiny of those threats, whether real or perceived, is in order.

DESIGN AND ORGANIZATION OF STUDIES IN PART I

Before I conduct in-depth evaluation of the impact of NCLB and state accountability policies on student outcomes in Part II, I address several underlying issues that arise at the intersection of accountability policy, research and practice in Part I.

As far as accountability is essential for improving the operation and performance of any human enterprise, including schools, we should guard against potential risks and threats to current federal and state educational accountability systems. Threats to the validity and legitimacy of test-driven external accountability policy may come from many sources. They may include challenges from new scientific research evidence that does not support the efficacy of accountability policy. Chapter 2 addresses this issue by conducting a meta-analysis of empirical studies. A threat may come from institutional realities of current public school systems such as limited resources and capacities of schools and teachers that constrain effective implementation of the policy. Chapter 3 addresses the issue of institutional threats to the implementation of accountability policy. Finally, a threat may arise from technical limitations and problems of current test measures that drive school accountability decision-making. Chapter 4 addresses technical threats to NCLB and states' performance-based accountability system.

CHAPTER 2

RESEARCH THREATS

Accountability Garners Mixed Evidence

There are controversies about whether external, test-driven accountability policy enhances or hinders academic achievement. NCLB calls for scientific evidence-based education policy. However, is current test-driven external accountability policy itself based on "scientific" research evidence? The case that drew the most attention was Texas, where the evidence on the effects of high-stakes testing on equity was mixed and often contradictory (Carnoy et al., 2001; Grissmer & Flanagan, 1998; Grissmer et al., 2000; Haney, 2000; Skrla et al., 2004; Valencia et al., 2004). While studies provide mixed or inconclusive evidence at best, only favorable research findings may be used to support the policy. This potential research bias may threaten the validity of accountability policy. Further, studies that evaluated the effect of high-stakes testing with each state's own benchmarks suffered from threats to generalization due to the lack of comparability of results with other states and potential risk of test score inflation over time.[1]

The past literature reviews have several limitations, generating more questions than answers on the effects of high-stakes testing and accountability (see Heubert, 2000; Langenfeld, Thurlow & Scott, 1996; NRC, 1999; Phelps, 2005). First, the reviews tended to be descriptive rather than meta-analytic. Second, the reviews were highly inclusive in their selection of relevant studies. A test was considered high stakes if the results of the test have perceived or real consequences for students, staff, or schools (Madaus, 1988). By including research based on this broad definition of high-stakes

The Testing Gap, pages 39–28
Copyright © 2007 by Information Age Publishing
All rights of reproduction in any form reserved.

testing, the reviews raised the issue of comparability of study findings. Third, the studies included in the past reviews did not fully capture recent changes in testing and accountability requirements; the studies examined mostly minimum competency tests for promotion and graduation, featuring their emphasis on basic skills and using students as the primary target of accountability. Finally, the studies in the past reviews were mostly restricted to samples from a single state or locality. Therefore, there is a growing need for reviewing this new line of research evidence to better inform the current educational policy debate.

This review focuses on cross-state causal-comparative and correlational studies that used national assessment data to evaluate the effects of external test-driven accountability on reading and/or mathematics achievement (see the list of studies in Appendix B). It is important to use an independent, low-stakes test such as NAEP to measure outcomes although the treatment is high-stakes testing. Therefore, studies using the state's own assessment measures are not included in this review. Studies using achievement measures drawn from nonrepresentative samples (such as SAT, ACT, and AP) for cross-state comparisons also are excluded. This review not only synthesizes findings through a meta-analysis of the "effect size" estimates from multiple studies but also examines key differences among the studies to account for variations in their findings. Methodological limitations of the studies are discussed, and some re-analyses are conducted to gain further insights into specific issues.

META-ANALYSIS: THE RELATIONSHIP BETWEEN TEST-DRIVEN ACCOUNTABILITY AND ACADEMIC ACHIEVEMENT

True experimental research with randomized assignment of the 50 states to high-stakes testing vs. low-stakes testing may not be possible. Given natural interstate variations in high-stake testing policy and academic achievement, however, the states provide an ideal laboratory for ex post facto policy research such as causal-comparative and correlational designs. Yet there has been relatively little research that has investigated the policy-outcome linkage at the state level. The decisive inhibiting factor has been the lack of good measures of state-level educational policies and achievement outcomes. With the advent of NAEP state assessment in the 1990s, the amount of research about which state education policies, if any, account for students' achievement gains on the NAEP has grown.

One of the first attempts in this line of research was Frederiksen (1994), which used long-term trend NAEP to estimate the effect of minimum competency testing (MCT) on state average math achievement gain scores.

The study's finding of significantly positive MCT policy effect was challenged later by Jacob (2001) who found from the analysis of NELS that the same policy had no significant impact on 12th grade reading and math achievement. A more mixed finding was given by Bishop and colleagues (2001) who reported that the effect of MCT alone was meager but the effect of curriculum-based end-of-course exams in combination with MCT was very strong.

Grissmer and Flagnan (1998) promoted discussion on school accountability policy effects by attributing substantial achievement gains on 1992–1996 NAEP in North Carolina and Texas to challenging student performance standards and test-driven accountability policies. This study was highly speculative and did not directly estimate the policy effects. Amrein and Berliner (2002) conducted a more extensive analysis of the policy-outcome linkages by tracking the performance of 18 states with a high-stakes testing system on NAEP, SAT and ACT measures. They claimed that the larger achievement gains in North Carolina and Texas was an "illusion arising from exclusion" and that the impact of high-stakes testing on student achievement is indeterminate.

The Amrein and Berliner study was challenged through subsequent reanalyses of the same policy and NAEP data by Raymond and Hanushek (2003), Rosenshine (2003), and Braun (2004). While all of the three studies were very critical of the original study on methodological grounds, Braun gave a more mixed picture of the policy effect. Raymond and Hanushek (2003) and Rosenshine (2003) produced highly positive results in favor of high-stakes testing policy. Amrein-Beardsley and Berliner (2003) conducted a further analysis in their response to Rosenshine's re-analysis to support their original finding. Carnoy and Loeb's (2002) study added new evidence with an analysis of the 1996–2000 NAEP achievement gains that supports the effectiveness of test-driven accountability policy: the observed policy effect was found consistently across racial and ethnic groups (White, Black, and Hispanic students) at both lower and upper NAEP achievement levels (Basic and Proficient).

Lee and Wong's study (2004) revealed more mixed results on accountability policy effects by differentiating the results for academic excellence versus equity. They found moderately positive policy effect on improving average math achievement but no significant effect on closing racial achievement gaps during the 1992–2000 period; Black and Hispanic students in strong accountability states did not make significantly greater achievement gains than did their White counterparts of the same socioeconomic status.

For the present meta-analysis, there was a total of 55 effect size estimates available from the 12 studies mentioned above that investigated the effects of statewide high-stakes testing and test-driven accountability policies on reading and/or mathematics achievement during the 1990s (see Appendix B). As shown in Appendix B, most studies reported multiple measures of policy effects because of their investigation of data from multiple grades, time periods and/or subject areas. Some studies were simply replication of prior studies using the same data but different methods. All of the studies looked at the average policy effects for all students. Only a few of them, including Lee and Wong (2004), Hanushek and Raymond (2004), and Carnoy and Loeb (2002), examined the effects by subgroups or the effects on the achievement gaps among subgroups.

Generally, six studies favored high-stakes testing states, five studies were mixed or insignificant, and one study favored low-stakes testing states. The average effect size from all 55 estimates turned out to be modestly positive, while the effect size varied substantially among the measures ranging from −.67 to 1.24 ($M = .36$, $SD = .45$). The average effect size can be highly misleading as it obscures substantial variations between and within the studies (see Figure 2.1). The distribution is not normal as there are some extreme cases with bipolarization of positive and negative effects. The between-study variation was significantly greater than the within-study variation; $F (11, 43) = 2.81$, $p < .01$. In the following sections, key factors that may have influenced variations in their effect sizes among the studies are discussed and analyzed using ANOVA.[2]

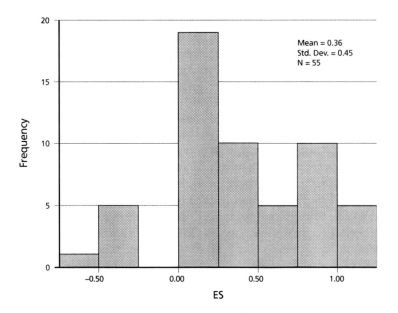

Figure 2.1.   Distribution of 55 effect size estimates from 12 cross-state causal-comparative and correlational studies on the effects of high-stakes testing and accountability policy on reading and math achievement.

Distribution of 55 effect size estimates from 12 cross-state causal-comparative and correlational studies on the effects of high-stakes testing and accountability policy on reading and math achievement.

FACTORS ACCOUNTING FOR VARIATIONS IN THE EFFECT SIZE ESTIMATES

Accountability Policy Variables

The effect size may vary among studies depending on the nature, type and timing of policy as an independent variable. The central question arises as to whether all of the studies actually used the same criteria for their classification of states as high vs. low-stakes testing or strong vs. weak accountability. In other words, did the studies define the "treatment" group in the same manners? Among 50 states, Amrein and Berliner's (2002) high-stakes testing policy index (the number of stakes attached to testing) is very positively correlated with Carnoy and Loeb's (2002) accountability index $r = .69$, $p < .01$) and with Lee and Wong (2004)'s accountability factor $r = .72$, $p < .01$). The correlation between Carnoy and Loeb's index and Lee and Wong's factor is stronger $r = .85$, $p < .01$), as the latter subsumes the former. Despite the evidence of convergent validity, not all studies examined the same construct of policy treatment.

By and large, the effect size appears to be relatively larger when the primary target of accountability policy are schools or a combination of schools and students rather than students alone ($M = .39$ for school accountability; $M = .38$ for student and school accountability combined; $M = .31$ for student accountability). However, this difference is not statistically significant; there were too few studies that investigated school accountability only.

It is not possible to disentangle the effects of a single particular policy from other policies adopted at the same time. Is it accountability policy only that had an impact on the achievement gains during the period of 1996–2000? When examining this question, the studies are vulnerable to model specification bias, that is, the omission of a confounding policy variable as a predictor of achievement gain. While some studies acknowledged that test-driven accountability policy is just one component of standards-based education reform, they did not investigate this issue. The exceptions are Braun (2004) and Lee and Wong (2004), both of which attempted to control for a broader measure of standards-based education reform policy. While both studies did not find any significant changes as a result of the control, this does not rule out any other rival explanations.

What is simply called accountability policy in some studies actually refers to test-driven or performance-based accountability policy. Although performance-based accountability policy became more popular during the 1990s, it was added onto input-based accountability policy instead of replacing it.[3] As many reform states were active in adopting both types of accountability policy during the 1990s, looking at only one type of accountability policy may result in an overestimation of the policy effect on student achievement.

The effect size tends to vary among studies by their time periods ($M = .48$ for late 1990s; $M = -.13$ for early 1990s; $M = .08$ for 1980s). The average effect size from studies covering the late 1990s (e.g., 1996–2000) was significantly larger than the average effect size from studies covering the 1980s or early 1990s (e.g., 1992–96) ($p = .002$). This trend may be attributable to the fact that the focus of high-stakes testing and accountability policy has shifted from ensuring minimum competency and basic skills for low-achieving students to high standards and proficiency for all students.

Does the timing of the accountability policy variable match the time frame of the achievement outcome variable to capture the hypothesized policy effect? There is a potential bias arising from not considering variation among states in the starting point and duration of their accountability policy. In evaluating the policy effect, most studies gave no explicit consideration of when the policies became effective and how long the students in the NAEP sample were exposed to the policies. Further complicating this state policy calibration is that some states may have revised their policies over time.

Differences in Student Achievement Outcome Variables

The effect sizes tend to vary among subjects, grades, and time periods chosen for the analysis of student achievement outcome variables. First, the accountability policy effect is greater for mathematics than for reading ($M = .38$ for math; $M = .29$ for reading). However, the mean difference is not statistically significant ($p = .56$). Direct comparison of the results between two subject areas needs caution because the NAEP results for reading covers only grade 4 over a relatively short time period (1994–98); the ending point of year 1998 may be too early to find effects even if they exist. Moreover, relatively few studies examined the effect of policy on reading achievement; some studies that dealt exclusively with math may have chosen to report only such highly significant results after the fact.

Secondly, comparison of the policy effect by grade level shows that the effect varies between grade levels ($M = .44$ for elementary school grades; $M = .35$ for middle school grades; $M = .03$ for high school grades). However, the difference between lower and upper grade results was not statistically significant ($p = .24$). Studies using NAEP (Frederiksen, 1994), NELS (Jacob, 2001) or SAT/ACT (Amrein & Berliner, 2002) did not lend support for the effect of high-stakes testing at the high school level.[4] Since the major target of high-stakes testing policies (e.g., high school exit exam) was often the high school population, this result appears to contradict an expectation of greater policy effect at the upper grade level.

Third, the effect size does not vary systematically by the length of time period for evaluating achievement gain ($M = .33$ for one-shot; $M = .40$ for 4-year gains; $M = .39$ for 8-year gains). The overall mean difference by the length of achievement gain is not statistically significant ($p = .96$). This results appears to be inconsistent with the expectation that longer exposure to a given policy as a treatment will generate more significant effects. There are potential threats to the validity of not only cross-sectional studies using achievement status in one particular year but also repeated cross-sectional studies that did not consider possible regression and trend artifacts in evaluating achievement gains for a limited time period.

Figure 2.2 shows state average performance trends from 1990 through 2000 in NAEP 8th grade mathematics as classified by Carnoy and Loeb's (2002) state accountability index. If we just look at the gains between 1996 and 2000, it is obvious that strong accountability states (4 and 5) made greater gains than did weak accountability states (0 and 1). Even after controlling for the differences in initial level of achievement (i.e., 1996 performance level) between strong and weak accountability states, Carnoy and Loeb found that the effect of accountability remained significant.

The 1990–2000 NAEP 8th grade math average score trends as classified by Carnoy and Loeb's (2002) accountability policy index (N = 1 state for

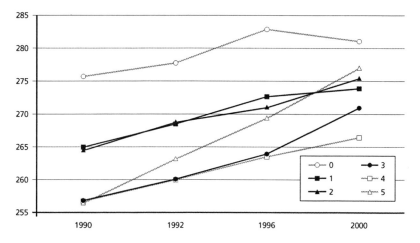

Figure 2.2.   1990–2000 NAEP 8th grade math average score trends as classified by Carnoy and Loeb (2002)'s accountability policy index (N= 1 state for index 0; N = 7 states for index 1, N = 4 states for index 2, N = 2 states for index 3, N = 5 states for index 4, N = 3 states for index 5).

index 0; N = 7 states for index 1, N = 4 states for index 2, N = 2 states for index 3, N = 5 states for index 4, N = 3 states for index 5).

Now if we look at the state performance trends prior to the 1996–2000 period, we gain a different insight into the policy-outcome linkage. No doubt strong accountability states (particularly in states with an accountability index of 5) have a relatively steeper performance trajectory (i.e., faster growth rate) throughout the 1990–2000 period. However, it is also apparent that the states with an index of 5 maintained the original rate of growth without any notable change between 1996 and 2000. The same is true for states with an accountability index of 4, which made relatively small gains but maintained their original growth rate throughout the period. In other words, the relatively larger achievement gains observed in strong accountability states appear to have started in the early 1990s, and perhaps, even earlier, before test-driven accountability policies were fully in place.

This trend data raises questions about the argument that strong accountability states' relatively larger achievement gains in the 1990s are attributable to their recent testing policy (beyond a regression effect). Moderate accountability states showed mixed patterns: states with an accountability index of 2 showed a linear growth pattern while states with an accountability index of 3 significantly increased growth during the 1996–2000 period by making greater achievement gains than they had previously. In contrast, weak accountability states (index of 0 and 1) made significant gains between 1990 and 1996 but made little or no gains between 1996 and 2000. What made the performance trend for those states flat during the 1996–2000 period? It is worth noting that the observed effect of accountability on the 1996–2000 gain does not result from increases in the academic growth of strong accountability states, but from the flattening of growth in weak accountability states.

Differences in the Analytic Samples

Schools and student samples were randomly selected in participating NAEP states. Although the random sampling of schools and students may help ensure the representation of their target populations within each state, there are potential biases in excluding certain groups of students including students with learning disabilities and English language learners. Since the exclusion rate of such students varied from state to state, Amrein and Berliner (2002) pointed out that the larger achievement gains in high-stakes testing states such as North Carolina and Texas are attributable partly to their relatively large increases in exclusion rates. For instance, there was a 10 percent increase for North Carolina and an 8 percent increase for Texas between 1992 and 2000 NAEP 4th grade math assessments. However, Braun (2004) showed that those two states are outliers that deviate from a general pattern: there was weak or no relationship between change in exclusion rate and gain scores among all participating NAEP states. In addition, in Carnoy and Loeb (2002) and Raymond and Haushek (2003), it appears that statistically adjusting gain scores for changes in exclusion rates did not lead to significant changes in the estimation of policy effects.

Finally, are observed gaps varying among different groups of students? Most studies examined the policy effect for all students. Only two studies disaggregated the results by racial group or examined the policy effects on racial achievement gaps. Carnoy and Loeb (2002) suggested that the effects are greater for Blacks and Hispanics than for Whites, particularly at Basic level, although the statistical significance of this difference was not tested in the analysis that analyzed each group separately. Lee and Wong (2004), who directly tested the racial differences in average growth rate, did not find a significant policy effect; in other words, the policy did not change racial achievement gaps. This discrepancy may be related to investigating a different time period and the list of control variables used in their models. The overall mean difference among 9 effect size measures by racial group ($M = .38$ for White; $M = .59$ for Black; $M = .70$ for Hispanic) is not statistically significant ($p > .05$).

Methods for Examining Policy-Outcome Linkages

Among the 55 effect size measures, fourteen came from cross-sectional studies, and forty-one from longitudinal or quasi-longitudinal studies. Seven of those forty-one estimates used a cohort-based tracking method for the analysis of achievement gain, whereas thirty-four of them used a grade-based or age-based successive group comparison method.

For example, the cohort-based method to examine states' academic improvement on NAEP over the 1996–2000 period was to compare NAEP scores from the 1996 4th grade with NAEP scores form the 2000 8th grade. As the NAEP used separate sampling procedures each year, there is no guarantee that the 1996 4th grade sample can be well matched to the 2000 8th grade sample. Nevertheless, the gain scores obtained through such a quasi-longitudinal tracking of the same cohort is more likely to be free from the cohort artifact.[5]

Figure 2.3 shows that the estimate of the policy effect is null for cohort-based analysis ($M = -.07$) but moderately positive for grade-based or age-based analysis ($M = .46$). The mean difference of .53 between the two methods is statistically significant ($p < .001$). One outlier in the distribution of cohort-based studies is Raymond and Hanushek's study. This sharp con-

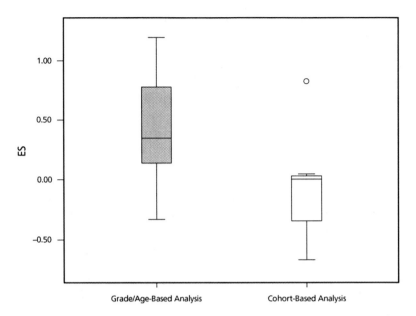

ES

Grade/Age-Based Analysis   Cohort-Based Analysis

Figure 2.3.   The distributions of accountability policy effect size estimates (ES) by analytical method (N = 7 for cohort-based gain score analysis method; N = 34 for grade/age-based gain score analysis method).

trast indicates that the results are highly sensitive to the choice of analytic method. Part of this difference between methods, that is, larger effect for grade-based comparison may be related to the time span of data used by each method, since a cohort-based comparison method affords only 4-year gain, whereas an age-based or grade-based method allows for longer time span (e.g., 10 years from 1990 to 2000).

The distributions of accountability policy effect size estimates (ES) by analytical method (N = 7 for cohort-based gain score analysis method; N = 34 for grade/age-based gain score analysis method).

Another critical research design factor that may have caused differences among the studies was the point of comparison, that is, what group of states is treated as a comparison group. Raymond and Hanushek (2003) criticized Amrein and Berliner's decision to compare high-stakes testing states with the national average instead of low-stakes testing states as a violation of a basic principle of scientific research. In fact, this choice made a difference in the average effect size estimates between Amrein and Berliner (2002) and subsequent re-analyses of the same data (*M* = .08 for Amrein and Berliner; *M* = .57 for the combination of studies including Braun; Raymond and Hanushek,; and Rosenshine).

Reporting and Interpretation of Policy Effects

Regardless of the choice of policy and achievement outcome variables, the studies also differed in their reporting and interpretation of statistical vs. practical significance of their findings. Grissmer and Flanagan (1998) and Amrein and Berliner (2002) did not report either statistical or practical significance. All other studies reported the statistical significance of concerned differences or relationships (p values) but not always the effect sizes.

How large of an effect is enough to declare a policy a success? There is no one-size-fits-all criterion to evaluate the size of a policy effect, and the studies also differed in their choice of a yardstick used for the effect size. For instance, Carnoy and Loeb (2002) did not directly report the effect sizes of accountability policy, but they referred to the standard deviation of state-level gain scores as a yardstick of the effect size by saying that "with a mean gain of 4.8 percentage points and a standard deviation of 3.6 in average state proportions scoring at or above basic skill levels, the increase in gain from raising the external pressure on schools by the state appears to be substantial." This statement can be misleading because most states made very small and insignificant gains that appear larger than they really are when interstate variations in gain scores are used as a criterion to evaluate the effects of a policy. Instead, Lee and Wong (2004) used the standard deviation of student-level test scores as an alternative yardstick to gauge the effect size. For a two-standard deviation increase in accountability policy score (i.e., changing from weak to strong accountability), their estimated mathematics score gain for all 8th grade students during the 1992–2000 period was about 10 points. This amount exceeds one standard deviation of the state-level gain scores but only one-third of the standard deviation of student-level scores. Clearly the policy effect sizes that were based on the distribution of state-level vs. student-level test scores are different.

Further, if we also evaluate the size of the reported policy effect relative to an announced policy goal (e.g., NCLB's goal of reaching 100 percent proficiency for all students by 2014), test-driven external accountability policy turns out to be far less effective. For White 8th graders in Carnoy and Loeb study, for example, a two-step move (e.g., shifting from simple testing requirements to having moderate repercussions for schools and districts in combination with a high school exit test) would bring about a 2.5 percentage point gain in the percentage of students meeting or exceeding Proficient level.

LIMITATIONS OF PRIOR STUDIES AND SUGGESTIONS FOR FUTURE DIRECTIONS

Since there has been a strong call for evidence-based education policy, the validation of studies requires that their findings stand up to rigorous scientific scrutiny (NRC, 2002; Slavin, 2002). The above-mentioned studies share several limitations. The biggest threats to internal validity of causal-comparative and correlational studies arise from non-random assignment of states to treatment (accountability policy in this case) that result in many unknown differences in the characteristics of subjects between experimental and comparison groups (see Campbell & Stanley, 1963). This threat to internal validity prevents us from confidently making causal attribution of states' achievement gains to their accountability policy.

Can we generalize the findings of studies to all states including non-NAEP states? Will the estimated effect of accountability policy show up in other unexamined subjects and grades as well? While the studies' use of a large-scale NAEP database with a statewide representative sample of students may contribute to its external validity, there are other potential limitations such as nonparticipating states, limited time periods, and selected grades and subjects that constrain the generalizability of the study findings. This problem may be ameliorated in future studies as the role and scope of NAEP has expanded to include all states with biennial testing as a result of NCLB. At the same time, however, NAEP may become less immune from the threat of test contamination as a result of its enhanced role to confirm state assessment results under NCLB.

The studies reviewed herein examined policy effects on achievement during the past two decades, but some policies may still be too recent to make measurable effects. Student accountability polices may have more immediate impact, such as academic promotion or graduation depending on test performance. School accountability policies may take longer. While states report on school performance, the reporting may not translate into real sanctions in immediate terms; there may be sanctions after 3–5 years of failing performance. In other words, accountability systems vary on the actual and immediate use of "high stakes" measures. If these are designed for a longer term purpose, then they are not likely to have any effects. Clearly, there is a need for evaluating the policy effect over the long run.

Whether high-accountability states averaged significantly greater gains on the NAEP test than students in states with little or no accountability measures, reasons for the presence or absence of an expected effect remains to be investigated and explicated fully. Previous studies tended to take a purely empirical or atheoretical approach in evaluating the effect of accountability. Most studies did not present any theoretical or conceptual framework about the mechanism through which accountability policy might have affected student outcomes.

CONCLUSION

This review was restricted to only cross-state causal-comparative and correlational studies which attempted to explore the effects of states' test-driven external accountability policy on students' academic achievement. The meta-analysis of 55 effect size estimates drawn from twelve selected studies showed a modestly positive policy effect on average but no significant effect on narrowing the racial achievement gap. Nevertheless, there is mixed evidence on the policy–outcome linkage, and the effect sizes tend to vary significantly between the studies. Educational policymakers and practitioners should be cautioned against relying exclusively on research that is consistent with their predetermined arguments for or against the current high-stakes testing policy movement. They should become aware of potential biases arising from the uncertainty and variability of evidence in the literature.

While NCLB calls for evidence-based education policy, the past research on the impact of test-driven accountability policy on achievement fell short of rigorous scientific research standards. Any causal attribution from such observational studies is not warranted because of many serious threats to internal validity. Past studies generally focused on the issue of whether high-stakes testing policy works or not, paying less attention to other important questions such as why or under what circumstance they may work. Without a conceptual framework of the policy-outcome linkage, studies cannot offer any plausible explanations for why accountability policy may or may not be related to improved achievement. To argue that states adopting strong accountability policies significantly improved student achievement is not convincing until substantial improvements in schooling conditions and practices occur. Moreover, any hidden costs and adverse side effects of high-stakes testing and accountability policy need further investigations.

Cross-state comparative and correlational studies can make a timely and important contribution to policy discussion by producing more generalizable knowledge on the effects of high-stakes testing policy based on common national assessment results for the comparison of student achievement outcomes. At the same time, however, they also raise the stakes for NAEP. Indeed, NAEP gains greater importance in the current accountability policy debate under NCLB as it is often seen as the single most reliable, valid, and readily available tool to compare states' academic status and progress and to possibly confirm states' own assessment results on student achievement in core subjects.

NOTES

1. Previous comparisons of the NAEP and state assessment results showed significant discrepancies in the level of student achievement as well as the size of statewide achievement gains (Klein et al., 2000; Koretz & Barron, 1998; Lee & McIntire, 2002; Linn et al., 2002). See chapter 8 in this book for details.

2. This meta-analysis using ANOVA may violate the assumption of the independence of observations for two reasons:(1) some of the studies re-analyzed the data from a previous study; and (2) multiple measures (e.g., reading and math) were drawn from the same studies (see Hedges, 1990 for discussion of statistical dependence among effect sizes). However, this potential problem has some qualifications. First, when multiple studies shared the same sample, they used independently chosen, different analytical methods to estimate the effects. Second, when multiple measures from the same study involved uses of a common method, the effects were estimated separately from independent samples (e.g., 4th grade vs. 8th grade samples).

3. Between 1985 and 1995, the number of states which used student assessment results for school accountability (school awards/recognition, performance reporting, or accreditation) increased from 26 to 39. During the same period, the number of states that used the test results for student accountability (student awards/recognition, promotion or graduation) slightly increased from 22 to 25 (Goertz, 1986; NCREL, 1996). But at the same time, the number of states which required passing exams for new teacher license has doubled between 1985 and 1996: from 13 to 29 in basic skills test, from 11 to 24 in professional knowledge test; from 14 to 24 in subject knowledge test (Goertz, 1986; CCSSO, 1996).

4. The use of college entrance exam scores such SAT and ACT to evaluate the effect of a high school exit exam can be misleading since a high school exit exam affects lower-achieving students most. Even if the exit exam could affect college-bound students' achievement as well, using SAT or ACT results for the analysis of their achievement gains is problematic because the trends are influenced by changes in the composition of test-takers.

5. While successive cohort comparison method that compares average student performance at the same grade level over time has been used widely in evaluating school-level academic growth, the volatility of gain scores obtained through this method is very severe (Kane & Staiger, 2002; Lee & Coladarci, 2002; Linn & Huag, 2002). Although this grade-based method should produce more reliable estimates of achievement gains at the state level, concerns about a cohort artifact confounding the gain estimates remain.

CHAPTER 3

INSTITUTIONAL THREATS

Accountability Meets School Realities

Test-driven school accountability under NCLB imposes new threats to schools and teachers so that they try to dodge or counteract the threats (Popham, 2004). There is often resistance to data collection and reporting, since it generates further push for accountability. Particularly, teachers tend to be very negative about high-stakes testing and school accountability policies (Leithwood, Steinbach, & Jantzi, 2002; Pupham, 2001; Sunderman, Kim, & Orfield, 2005). Teachers often perceive statewide tests as placing increased demands on their overcrowded schedule, and find no substantial added benefits for students (Wilson & Corbett, 1990). A common conception among school administrators and teachers is that professional growth and teacher accountability are either incompatible objectives, or goals that must be accomplished separately. However, the ignorance or sabotage of external accountability for the cause of professional growth may lead into the "professionalism trap," with possible backfire from policymakers, parents and the media that demand measurable results from schools. Polls show that the public has been largely in favor of high-stakes testing (Phelps, 2005).

How does top-down, test-driven external school accountability work in a multi-layered school system? How do teachers respond to the policy mandate in their loosely coupled school organizations? Past policy implementation research focused primarily on variations in the response of individuals and institutions, and on the conditions of successful implementation. The

The Testing Gap, pages 53–65
Copyright © 2007 by Information Age Publishing

Rand Agent Study, for example, concluded that successful implementation is characterized by a process of mutual adaptation in which project goals and methods are modified to suit the needs and interests of local staff and in which that staff changed to meet the requirements of the project (McLaughlin, 1976). Yet implementation research has come under increasing criticism for its lack of parsimonious theory that specifies in any systematic way the relationship among the policy problems being addressed, the basic design features of a policy, the implementing organization, and the political and organizational context in which policy targets must respond (McDonnell & Elmore, 1987).

Because standards-based reform and accountability policies initiated by the federal government and states during the last two decades are distinctive in all of these aspects, previous implementation models based on discrete, redistributive federal programs may not fit the case of comprehensive, developmental policies. First, while the primary policy goal of American education system shifted from equality of educational opportunity to academic excellence, the notion of performance-driven accountability has become institutionalized throughout the system. Second, as many states shifted to the use of more powerful strategies aimed at changing instructional practices, the governance structure of state education systems has become more centralized with regard to curricular and instructional decision-making. Finally, as a result of improvement of educational technology and enhanced capacity to inspect educational productivity, schools now face much stronger demand for technical performance without also experiencing a decline in demands for institutional conformity (Rowan & Miskel, 1999).

In light of these concerns, this chapter explores institutional and organizational threats to standards-based education reform and accountability policies. School context and teacher professionalism may shape the extent to which test-driven accountability policies are implemented. As a result, state policymakers in strong accountability states may have faced problems such as local resistance, non-implementation, and goal displacement during the process of top-down school reform. Building on the literature review, I explore a model of educational policy implementation in which the characteristics (goals, instruments, benefits and costs) of state education policies interact with the context (values, power, climate and capacity) of schools to influence teaching and learning outcomes.

KEY CHARACTERISTICS
OF STATE ACCOUNTABILITY POLICY

Standards-based education reform and test-driven accountability policies adopted during the past two decades can be described in terms of the following characteristics: policy goals, policy instruments, policy benefits/ costs, and potential risks (see Table 3.1).

TABLE 3.1
The Characteristics of Standards-based Education Reform and Accountability Policies

	Policy type	
	Student-oriented	Teacher-oriented
Policy goals	Enhance overall quality of student learning and achievement for academic excellence	Enhance systemwide teacher quality for improving teaching and student achievement
Policy mechanism (instruments)	Raising standards for academic performance, promotion and high school graduation (course credit, exit test, attendance) ➤ Use mandate and/or inducement to regulate the promotion and exit of students (gatekeeping)	Raising standards for teacher qualification, education and (re)certification (GPA, skills test, observation) ➤ Use mandate and/or inducement to control the entry of individuals into the teaching profession (gatekeeping)
Policy benefits/costs	Benefits: Increase student exposure to more rigorous curriculum/assessment and help all students meet high performance standards Costs: Reduce costs through ready-made standardized tests and transfer costs of support to LEAs and schools	Benefits: Increase student access to better qualified teachers and help teachers improve learning outcomes for all students Costs: Diffuse costs to several stakeholders (i.e. IHEs, LEAs, schools) accountable for different stages of teacher training
Potential risks	Make socioeconomically disadvantaged minority students drop out of schools rather than help them meet high standards Exacerbate the achievement gap by having more advantaged students (who otherwise would stay in schools needing improvement) move to high-achieving schools through transfer options	Screen out false negatives rather than develop the talents of those who wish to become and remain teachers Worsen school performance disparities by having more qualified teachers (who otherwise would stay in schools needing improvement) move to high-achieving schools due to the threat of sanctions

First, policy goals refer to ultimate values or goals which policymakers intend to accomplish through concrete policy actions. During the last decade, there has been a subtle shift in the basic goals of the American education system from an emphasis on equity and freedom of access to concern for quality education and academic excellence (Mitchell et al., 1990). The basic skills emphasis of the 1960s and 1970s has been challenged in many local districts and states which have instituted reforms emphasizing higher order thinking and a more challenging curriculum (O'Day & Smith, 1993).

However, there are tenuous links between the goals set by the reform reports and their actual recommendations and even more tenuous links between the recommendations and changes in the schools (Ginsberg & Wimpelberg, 1987). Moreover, the imperatives of centralized educational policymaking may have led to a substantially narrower view of the purposes of education. As policies are more and more centrally determined, abstract and salutary goals are reduced and trivialized, and only those goals which can be measured are implemented. It is argued that the exigencies of the policymaking process, together with the limited technology for making policies, causes "goal reduction" (Wise, 1979).

Secondly, policy instruments refer to the ways in which policies are designed to be implemented. This involves decision-making on what policy instruments are used to accomplish the adopted policy goals. McDonnell and Elmore (1987) proposed four generic classes of policy instruments: mandates, inducements, capacity-building, and system-changing. Many times the imposition of new mandates seems the most feasible option because it appears relatively inexpensive and presumably sends a clear signal about what policymakers expect from those being regulated. Inducements like grants-in-aid are most often used when policy must move through the intergovernmental system or when consensus about the change that needs to occur is low. Indeed, state policymakers have relied primarily on regulation and/or inducements as their major policy instruments (Elmore & Fuhrman, 1995).

Capacity-building and system-changing are more challenging than mandates and inducements in terms of implementation problems and expected effects. Capacity-building captures those policies that focus mainly on longer-term developmental objectives rather than on short-term compliance or production. The notion of transfers of authority underlying system-changing captures a common problem confronted by policymakers—how to match purposes with existing or potential institutions. As the states move to performance-driven school reform, there have been many attempts to build the capacities of schools and teachers and/or to redistribute power among the layers of the school system. However, states' successful use of these challenging policy instruments requires a fundamental rethinking and restructuring of the process of schooling—decentralization, profession-alization, and bottom-up change (Smith & O'Day, 1991). Consequently, states are exhibiting no clear shift in school reform direction, and the easi-est-to-implement reforms have stayed in place (Danzberger et al., 1992).

Thirdly, policy benefit/cost concerns the costs and benefits of policy implementation. Little attention has been paid to the financial or proce-dural requirements for putting policy recommendations into practice (Ginsberg & Wimpelberg, 1987). The number of "unfunded" initiatives and/or the relatively low magnitude of dedicated funds for education reform policies and programs indicate that numerous education reform initiatives have been leveraged through lump-sum funding increases (Jor-dan & McKeown, 1990). Thus, it is difficult to determine whether addi-tional funding is for reform or maintenance of different programs. Likewise, the expected benefits of a particular education policy are diffi-cult to figure out because legislative school reform packages include many policies that considered the effects of change on the total system (Under-wood, 1989).

State education policy has been poorly defined in terms of who is responsible for implementing the policy and who is expected to benefit from the outcomes. When there are no clear beneficiaries of policy and no clear targets of accountability, policies are less likely to be implemented successfully. As policies move down to the school and classroom levels, the success of policy implementation often depends on how implementors see policy benefits relative to their costs. For example, mandates require enforcement, and enforcement is costly to the enforcing agency as well as to the objects of enforcement. Policy costs include not only direct outlays but all opportunity costs, some of which are implicit rather than explicit costs. Teachers who are required to do more paperwork as a result of new state policies are less likely to prepare for their instruction (see Murphy, 1990). The benefits of complying with policy mandates sometimes accrue to policy implementors as well as to the target clientele or society as a whole. Teachers may feel that they can benefit from implementing high school graduation requirements for students (e.g., gaining more control over student behavior and working in orderly classrooms). Therefore, the cost-benefit ratio as perceived and assessed by policy implementors is criti-cal for policy implementation.

Is the current test-driven accountability policy efficient in terms of its cost-benefit ratio? Despite the argument that high-stakes testing is relatively cheaper than any other interventions and it produces a bigger bang for buck, federal and state governments do not consider the cost of full accountability. As states are expanding tests into more grades under NCLB and pushing for faster scoring and reporting at the same time, the future costs of testing and scoring are likely to exceed what they can afford

(Olson, 2005a).[1] One issue for school is lack of enough staff members to administer the tests and to provide accommodations such as more time and alternate settings. Further, the feds and states may attempt to transfer or diffuse the actual cost of implementation to others such as Local Education Agencies (LEAs) and schools which are held accountable for helping their students pass promotion or exit tests, and to the Institutions of Higher Education (IHEs), teacher education programs in particular, which are held responsible for ensuring that their students pass teacher certification exams.

CONTINGENCIES OF EDUCATIONAL POLICY IMPLEMENTATION

In the previous section, educational policy was described in terms of three attributes: goals, instruments and costs/benefits. Top-down school reform policies are likely to interact with the institutional and organizational contexts of the school systems to affect policy implementation and ultimately policy outcomes. As a unit, a school has a definable group of administrators and teachers that collectively determine organizational climate and capacity and play a major role in implementing educational policies. This contingency perspective is based on the assumption that policy implementation is a dynamic organizational process of interactions between top-down policy forces and bottom-up organizational responses.

When each of the nested hierarchical layers of the school system has a conditional and contributory relation to events and outcomes occurring at adjacent ones (Barr & Dreeben, 1983), even well-coordinated reform policies are not expected to automatically lead to desired policy implementation. On the one hand, there are mechanisms that coordinate or control the flow of policies and practices within the school system. Reforms that are isomorphic with the fundamental tenets of the institutional environment stand a better chance of survival than reforms that are not (Cuban, 1992; Meyer & Rowan, 1978; Rowan, 1982). On the other hand, there are also relationships at each level of the educational system that coordinate the technical aspects of delivering services. The distribution of resources necessary for learning forges vertical connections among the system's hierarchy of offices (Barr & Dreeben, 1988; Gamoran & Dreeben, 1986; Wong, 1994). When each state education system as a whole has its own collective identity in normative, structural, and functional aspects, the central question is: under what conditions do states effectively combine a centralized vision with local responsibility?

In this section, I describe a model of educational policy implementation where the fidelity of policy implementation depends upon the fit or convergence between policy characteristics and organizational conditions (see Figure 3.1). This model postulates that policy implementation is an interactive, dynamic process, that is, original policies can be modified and adjusted over time in a way to meet the demands and needs of implementors who also can modify their behaviors in response to changing policy mandates. Thus, from a long-term perspective, any discrepancy between the expected and realized outcomes of a policy may narrow if a process of mutual adaptation takes place effectively.

First, policy implementation depends on the congruence between policy goals and organizational values. In other words, the more policy goal is accepted and shared by educators, the better chances that they are to implement the reform policies. Loose linkage between policy goals and professional values in education has been suggested; teachers tend to translate formal goals into personalized objectives (see Jackson, 1968; Lortie, 1975). Elaborate and formalized student standards often fato be meaningful to teachers because the outcomes described in such standards may not ne those that teachers personally value (Rowan, 1996). If teacher certification and evaluation policies are designed to provide an operational basis for assessing competence for entry, for defining functional specificity of performance, and for circumscribing authority, teachers are not likely to readily accept such a rationalistic characterization of their roles (Wise, 1979).

Despite the alleged disjuncture between the rationalistic model of education and the reality of life in the classroom and variation among teachers

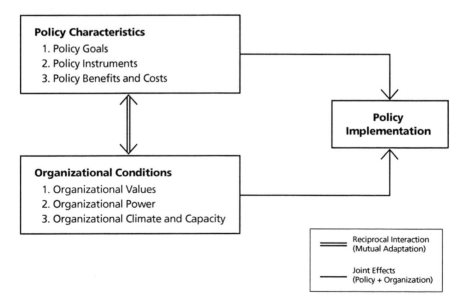

Figure 3.1.   Contingency model of educational policy implementation.

in their adoption of stated goals, a process of mutual adaptation between policymakers and implementors has been observed during policy implementation (McLaughlin, 1976; Peterson, Rabe, & Wong, 1986). At the initial stage of policy implementation, ambiguity of policy goal has an important function for policymakers and administrators because it allows them to hold people with different interests (Elmore, 1976). As the input-oriented reforms of the early 1980s become irrelevant to instructional changes in classrooms, state policymakers refined their policy goals to get renewed support for content-driven or performance-driven reform. As a result, the notion of "high academic standards for all students" became institutionalized throughout the system, overcoming an organizational affinity for curriculum differentiation and professional autonomy. Teachers who are already predisposed to teach content prescribed by state policies are more likely to realize their expectations about curriculum and pedagogy (see Archbald & Porter, 1994). Thus, from a longer-term policy implementation perspective, any differences between proposed policy goals and prevailing professional values that exist at the time of policymaking may recede over time, depending on the process of mutual adaptation.

Secondly, policy implementation also depends on the compatibility between policy instruments and organizational power. Top-down mandate would work more effectively in more centralized school system. Power in a multi-layered state education system is distributed to the degree to which state policymakers enable lower levels of policy actors, bureaucrats, and educators to implement policies. Given the regulatory nature of reform policies, highly centralized decisionmaking may be more favorable to ensuring compliance with policy directives than decentralized decision-making. By attributing policy dissonance among the educational system's organizational levels to dispersed authority over school practices, previous perspectives conceptualize public education as a loosely coupled system, a system composed of fairly insular organizational subunits (see Bidwell, 1965; Weick, 1976).

Despite the defining characteristics of loosely coupled systems, important changes in the organizational structure of schools have been observed that rendered them much more receptive to rationalistic, mandated changes than in the past (Murphy, Hallinger, & Mesa, 1985). New theoretical perspectives on organizational coupling also admit that symbolic and strategic factors guide policymaking by manifesting themselves in the structure, and organizational characteristics of schools (Loveless, 1993). Thus, from a long-term policy implementation perspective, a convergence between designed policy mechanisms and systemwide governance structure may evolve over time depending on the process of mutual adaptation.

Finally, policy implementation depends on the extent to which policy benefits and costs match organizational climate and capacity. Teachers who work in unfavorable school conditions (e.g., large class size and poor salary) and are not satisfied with their current job are less likely to implement top-down state policies unless the policies give them enough incentives to do so. The earlier policies such as new course requirements adopted by the states during the 1980s were clear-cut and easy-to-implement so that they hardly required increased motivation and effort from teachers. However, standards-based reform policies provided few incentives for teachers, in disadvantaged urban schools which suffer the lack of safe and orderly learning environment and collective support for education. Further, the school's current capacity for academic improvement (e.g., instructional resources, teacher qualifications and training) may constrain policy implementation when the policy demands upgrading instructional practices without sufficient funding, technical assistance and professional development (see Darling-Hammond & Post, 2000; Newmann & Wehlage, 1995).[2]

ORGANIZATIONAL CONTEXT OF SCHOOLS UNDER TEST-DRIVEN EXTERNAL ACCOUNTABILITY

In the context of state activism in education reform, policy implementation is depicted as a function of fit between major policy characteristics and corresponding school organizational factors. Building on the contingency model of educational policy implementation as depicted in Figure 3.1, I match a state policy variable with aggregate school organizational variables at the state level. The measure of state "activism" in test-driven external accountability as constructed by Lee and Wong (2004) is used; A higher score meant that the state was more active in adopting test-driven external accountability policies for schools, teachers, and students (see Chapter 1 of this book). In order to explore the relationship of this policy variable with school context variables, I identify and measure professional values, power, climate and capacity. Although there exist variations among individual schools, it is assumed that there are also institutional forces that lead to organizational homogeneity within the same state (DiMaggio & Powell, 1991).[3] The data are drawn from the 1993–94 Schools and Staffing Survey (SASS)[4] and 1996 NAEP school administrator survey (see Appendix C for description of the variables). Table 3.2 shows correlations between state accountability policy variable and school organizational context variables among 50 states.

First, the compatibility of policy goals with professional values is critical to successful policy implementation. As state education priorities shifted from basic skills to academic excellence during the last decade, state policies are more likely to be implemented in states where educators place a greater emphasis on academic excellence. As seen in Table 3.2, the correla-

TABLE 3.2
Correlations between State Accountability Policy Activism and School Organizational Context Variables (*N* = 50 states)

	State Activism in Test-Driven Accountability
1. Organizational Values (Priority of Educational Goals)	
Basic Skills as Top Priority	−.05
Academic Excellence as Top Priority	.38**
Personal Growth as Top Priority	−.30**
Human Relations as Top Priority	−.26
2. Organizational Power (Locus of Educational Control)	
Principal Influence on Curriculum	−.40***
Teacher Influence on Curriculum	−.52***
Principal Influence on Hiring Teachers	−.24
Teacher Influence on Hiring Teachers	−.42**
3. Organizational Climate and Capacity (Quality of Teaching Conditions)	
Safe and Orderly School Climate	−.45**
Collective Support for Education	−.66***
Teacher Commitment (Plan to Remain in Teaching)	−.26
Teacher Qualification (In-Field Teaching)	−.30*

Note: * $p < .05$; ** $p < .01$; *** $p < .001$.

tion between state accountability and school priority of educational goals is significantly positive academic excellence ($r = .38$), but negative for personal growth ($r = -.30$). This suggests that teachers in strong accountability states tend to place relatively heavy emphasis on academic excellence as most important educational goal but relatively light emphasis on whole-person development goal. Although the correlations do not allow us to draw any causal inferences, the relationships are likely to be reciprocal. While teachers' values may have influenced policy goals, test-driven accountability policies may have narrowed educational goals to improving academic achievement. It is also possible that both policy and teacher variables have been influenced by a third variable (e.g., statewide educational culture). Consequently, strong accountability states where teachers prioritized academic goals may have pursued achievement-oriented education at the risk of neglecting whole-person education.

Secondly, the fit between the school governance structure and the policy mechanisms used affects policy implementation. As the state education department becomes actively engaged in reform activities such as designing tests, establishing curriculum guides, and assisting and monitoring districts, state policies are more likely to be implemented in states where educators view the state department's curricular influence as more legitimate. As seen in Table 3.2, the correlation between state accountability and professional power is significantly negative ($r = -.40$ for principal influence on curriculum; $r = -.52$ for teacher influence on curriculum; $r = -.41$ for teacher influence on hiring teachers). Principals and teachers in strong accountability states tend to have relatively smaller influence on curricular and hiring decisions. This indicates that, in strong accountability states, decision-making authority is centralized in the state bureaucracy rather than at the school sites. This may have promoted compliance with top-down reform policy at the risk of discouraging bottom-up changes.

Finally, the implementation of test-driven accountability policies can be facilitated or constrained by the prevailing conditions of schools as a professional workplace for teachers. Table 3.2 shows that the correlations between state accountability and school climate/capacity variables are largely negative ($r = -.45$ for safe and orderly climate; $r = -.66$ for collective support; $r = -.26$ for teacher qualification; $r = -.30$ for teacher commitment). This suggests that the school conditions in strong accountability states are relatively unfavorable to teachers; their lower qualification for teaching and dissatisfaction with their workplace or job as a profession can negatively affect policy implementation. On the other hand, schools and teachers in strong accountability states may want to capitalize external accountability policy to improve schooling conditions. While clear-cut, low-cost, and easy-to-implement state education policies may have contributed to short-term policy conformity, the ultimate impact of these policies on instructional practices and student outcomes depends on school capacity-building and climate improvement efforts which can help overcome the relatively poor teaching environment in strong accountability states.

SUMMARY AND DISCUSSION

Given state activism in standards-based education reform during the last decade, the central questions are: how did different levels of the state education system respond to state educational policymaking, and how were values and resources used to produce policy outcomes? While most commission reports and reform policies focused on the environmental context of policymaking, there were few clear considerations of the organizational context of schools and the role of teachers as professionals that are crucial for successful translation of policy goals into student outcomes.

To better understand the effects of federal and state educational accountability policies, we need to understand how the institutional and organizational contexts of the multi-layered school system operate on the implementation of state education reform. The findings of this chapter show distinctive institutional and organizational context of accountability policies and point out potential threats to systemic policy implementation. First, teachers' reports about the priority of educational goals indicate that strong accountability states place a greater emphasis on academic values than on human caring practices. Secondly, principals' reports about the distribution of curricular influence indicate that strong accountability states empower the state department of education at the cost of weakening school-based management. Finally, principals' and teachers' reports about school conditions indicate that strong accountability states enforce cost-effective changes on their relatively disadvantaged schools without providing adequate incentives and support.

While test-driven external accountability policies are considered achievement-oriented, regulatory, and low-cost, these policy characteristics may "fit" with the school systems that prioritize academic goals, centralize the distribution of power, and operate schools like a factory rather than a professional workplace for teachers. In fact, these conditions may well characterize the first generation accountability states which were active in high-stakes testing well in advance of NCLB. But when the federal government tried to spread this policy to all states through NCLB, the policy may not transfer well due to very different schooling conditions and teacher/student needs in the second-generation states. The key challenge of the second-generation states under NCLB is to formulate desired connections between emerging test-driven external accountability policies and the long-standing institutional/organizational contexts of school systems for adaptations. Future in-depth case studies could address the question of how institutional and organizational threats to policy implementation can be transformed into opportunities in the long run.

NOTES

1. The estimate of testing cost depends on the type of tests used. The Government Accountability Office estimated that it would cost states $1.9 million to meet the testing requirements under NCLB over the six years of the federal law's authorization if they relied solely on multiple-choice questions that could be machine scored. But the cost would increase to $3.9 billion with a mix of multiple-choice and constructed-response items, and up to $5.3 billion with hand-scored, written responses (Olson, 2005a).

2. According to the National School Boards Association (2006), Congress has continued a steady decline in fully funding NCLB, shifting a greater portion of the cost of compliance with adequate yearly progress and supplemental services, for example, to local school districts and states. Since 2001, funding for Title I has increased by roughly 45 percent. However, these increases

were offset by rising costs due to enrollment increases and school programming that is needed to ensure students will meet the requirements of NCLB (e.g. class-size reduction, summer school, and professional development of teachers). Further, the cost to recruit and retain highly qualified teachers and paraprofessionals, as required by NCLB, continues to grow.

3. DiMaggio and Powell (1991) identify three mechanisms through which institutional isomorphic change occurs: (1) coercive isomorphism that stems from political influence and the problem of legitimacy; (2) mimetic isomorphism resulting from standard responses to uncertainty; and (3) normative isomorphism, associated with professionalization. While this analysis focuses on interstate variation in the state-level aggregate tendency of professional values, urban-suburban differences within the same state can be substantial: teachers who work with educationally disadvantaged minority students in inner-city schools are likely to develop different educational priorities (see McLaughlin, 1991).

4. The Schools and Staffing Survey (SASS) offers researchers the opportunity to study teachers' and principals' attitudes, behaviors, and conditions on a much larger scale than that afforded by the smaller scale or case study research typically available.

CHAPTER 4

TECHNICAL THREATS

Accountability Falls into Testing Traps

NCLB requires that schools make "adequate yearly progress" (AYP) towards the goal of having 100 percent of their students become proficient by year 2013–14. A stated goal of the NCLB accountability system is to provide accurate and meaningful information to the public on the quality of public schools and to identify schools with needs for academic improvement and intervention. The state department of education web site usually provides publicly available information on school average performance and progress that can be used as official measures of AYP. However, information on the reliability and validity of school accountability decision-making is not readily available. Validity concerns the interpretation and use of a test measure rather than a test itself, and it requires multiple sources of evidence. Most importantly, the validation of a test itself does not necessarily lead to valid decision-making for school accountability. When a test is used for school accountability purposes, it is no longer valid simply by virtue of its appropriate coverage of curriculum that students have learned. This is very much like the case that the validity of research involving causal attribution of effects requires evidence beyond instrumental validity. Therefore, the validity of school accountability systems goes beyond simple validation of assessment tools used and depends upon how well the construction, use, and interpretation of the AYP measure accomplishes the policy goal (see Marion et al., 2002).

The Testing Gap, pages 67–60

This leads to an important distinction between two test score interpretations: (1) do the scores represent the degree of individual students' standards attainment?; (2) do the scores represent how well the school has achieved its NCLB goals? The scores can possess a sufficient degree of validity for one interpretation but not the other. Information on the reliability and validity of a high-stakes test is often buried in an overwhelmingly complex technical report. The U.S. Department of Education required states to submit reliability and validity evidence of their standards-based student assessments. Although this federal review puts state tests under scrutiny, it focuses on standards and tests themselves but does not look into the issue of whether they are used appropriately and fairly for school accountability decision-making. In this chapter, I start with discussion of test scores as indicators of students' achievement of standards first, and then discuss reliability and validity of AYP indicators as measures of school accountability. All of these questions are examined with a focus on two selected states, Kentucky and Maine: the Kentucky Instructional Results Information System (KIRIS) and the Maine Educational Assessment (MEA). Kentucky is one of the strong accountability states, whereas Maine is one of the weak accountability states.

PSYCHOMETRIC PROPERTIES OF STATE ASSESSMENTS

Reliability is seen as a prerequisite for validity. Table 4.1 shows two types of reliability estimates for the NAEP and state assessments: internal consistency and interrater agreement. Both reliabilities are very high and they are acceptable. Efforts were made to maximize the reliability of scoring among different raters. For the MEA, steps included the preparation of a unique scoring guide for every question, the use of training and qualifying packets, scoring training itself, and the continual monitoring of scorers' work (MDE, 1995). A similar procedure was used for the KIRIS (KDE, 1997).

However, the above reliability estimates of NAEP and state test measures at the student level does not guarantee reliability of school aggregate measures at the school level. Current state accountability system usually employs a design that allows us to evaluate performance gains only at the school level through successive cohort comparison. While state assessment is administered at multiple grade levels every year, it does not keep track of the same students' academic progress over time. Even if a student remains in the same school system and his or her achievement can be tracked over time, the scale score and performance standard at different grades are not likely to be comparable. The nature of repeated cross-sectional assessment design does not facilitate vertical equating and linking performance standards from one grade to the next grade.

TABLE 4.1

Reliability of the 1996 NAEP, 1995 MEA and 1996 KIRIS 4th and 8th Grade Mathematics Assessments

| | | Reliability | |
Grade	Assessment	Internal Consistency (Cronbach's alpha coefficient)	Interrater Agreement (Correlation between the first and second raters)
4	NAEP	.95	.96
	MEA	.80	.89
	KIRIS	.81	.97
8	NAEP	.91	.96
	MEA	.80	.95
	KIRIS	.85	.99

Source:

Kentucky Department of Education (1997). *KIRIS Accountability Cycle 2 Technical Manual.* Median coefficient alpha based on common and matrix items across 12 forms.

N.L. Allen, J.E. Carlson, and C.A. Zelenak (1999). *The NAEP 1996 Technical Report.* Proportion of variance due to student sampling. This corresponds to reliability coefficient in classical test theory.

Maine Department of Education (1995). *Maine Educational Assessment 1994-95 Questions and Answers.* Interrater agreement rate for MEA was based on the 1999 MEA results.

Current state tests are argued to be valid based on the fact that they are well aligned with state's curriculum standards (content validity) and also that their scores are highly correlated with scores from other well-established standardized tests of the same construct (criterion validity).

Test specifications (test blueprints) provide information on the content validity of national and state assessments. Both Maine and Kentucky assessments modeled their frameworks closely after NAEP. One way to verify whether national and state assessments measure the same construct is to compute correlations between test scores from students who took both tests. The analyses of school average math test scores from the 1996 NAEP data in conjunction with the 1996 state assessment datasets showed a strong, positive relationship between NAEP and state assessment results in Maine and Kentucky. The school-level correlation between 1996 NAEP and state math scores was .50 (grade 4) and .52 (grade 8) in Kentucky and .63 (grade 4) and .70 (grade 8) in Maine.[1]

One may assume that because state standards were similar to the NAEP framework and as there was a reasonably high correlation between NAEP and state assessment results, the assessment content would be sufficiently similar and the performance could be compared directly. Even with similarities in standards, however, there can still be important differences between the assessments that lead to curricular and instructional variations.[2] Moreover, there is no single established criterion to determine the validity of an achievement test. Using correlations among related test measures as an evidence of test validity may fall into the fallacy of circular argument for validation.

RELIABILITY AND VALIDITY OF SCHOOL
ACCOUNTABILITY MEASURES

Previous studies have pointed out some critical problems with school AYP measures (Hill, 1997; Lee & Coladarci, 2002; Lee, 2003; Lee, 2004b; Linn & Haug, 2002; Thum, 2002), which foreshadow technical challenges for school accountability policy under NCLB. In this chapter, major threats to the validity of school accountability measures, including reliability, fairness and comprehensiveness, are discussed in the context of the AYP requirement under NCLB.

First, are school accountability test measures reliable? If the AYP measure changes too much by chance, it will no longer be consistent and accurate and thus it will threaten the validity of decisions based on the measure. Second, are school accountability test measures fair? If the AYP formula treats unequal schools equally, it will render the outcomes inequitable and lessen the validity of decisions about rewards and/or sanctions. Third, are school accountability measures comprehensive? If the AYP evaluation relies on a single test measure or a very limited set of outcome measures, it may bring bias into holistic judgment about school performance.

ARE SCHOOL ACCOUNTABILITY MEASURES RELIABLE?

Is the current state test measure of school performance reliable? I illustrate this issue with data from schools in Kentucky and Maine using 8th grade mathematics assessments: the KIRIS for 1993–1998 and the MEA for 1990–1998. MEA scores range from 100 to 400, with a mean of 250 and standard deviation of 50. The KIRIS accountability index score is a weighted composite reflecting the percentage of students at four different achievement levels (0 for Novice, .4 for Apprentice, 1.0 for Proficient, and 1.4 for Distinguished). Thus, KIRIS accountability index scores can range from 0 to 140. Correlations among the school average scores of 8th grade math achievement are moderately positive; the correlation between adjacent year scores are in the range of .5–.7, and they become weaker for remote years (Lee & Coladarci, 2002). These results indicate that school-level aggregate scores are not highly stable, and this stability lessens appreciably over the long term—the phenomenon of proximal autocorrelation in the time-series data (Campbell & Kenny, 1999).

Figure 4.1 illustrates two randomly selected schools in Maine (one from a rural area and another from an urban area). This rural school shows enormous volatility in its average math achievement score throughout the 1990–98 period, which makes it hard to detect its overall performance trend. In contrast, this urban school shows a greater degree of stability with its generally upward performance trend. Perhaps this difference in performance trend reflects their differences in school size and student composition.

Under the NCLB AYP provisions, schools have the option of "using a uniform averaging procedure, which is designed to mitigate the fact that student performance can vary widely from year to year due to factors beyond a school's control" ("Raising the Bar," 2002). Under this provision, schools can average test scores from the current school year with test scores from the preceding two years. This works in a school's favor when test scores decline but it works against a school when scores rise. One can assume that the rolling average procedure was used by schools only when they obviously benefitted from the option (i.e., when school performance declined). Nevertheless, whether states would actually allow schools to use the rolling average option in such a flexible way remains an open question (see Erpenbarch et al., 2003 for examples of state plans).

Applying the current AYP goal and timeline (100% proficient within 12 years) retrospectively to the past school performance data (1993–98 in

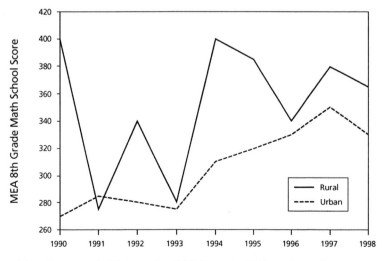

Figure 4.1.   Two sample Maine schools' 8th grade MEA math performance trajectories.

TABLE 4.2
Percentage of Maine and Kentucky Schools that Would Meet AYP Target without vs. with Use of "Rolling Average" Option

Year	Maine			Kentucky		
	No Rolling	Rolling	Odds	No Rolling	Rolling	Odds
1	100.0			80.4		
2	44.3	46.0	1.07	66.1	69.5	1.17
3	10.5	12.7	1.24	61.4	62.8	1.06
4	5.9	7.2	1.24	35.9	39.5	1.17
5				28.3	30.5	1.11
6				10.3	10.9	1.07

Note: Odds is the ratio of given percentages, i.e., the ratio of the probability of schools' meeting AYP target for all students each year with rolling average to their corresponding probability of passing without rolling average option.

Kentucky and 1995–98 in Maine), a study showed that the rolling average option would contribute to improvement of the reliability but little help to the feasibility of passing (Lee, 2004b). The percentage of schools that would meet their AYP target overall turned out to decrease exponentially over the course of the first few years (see Table 4.2). In Kentucky, it was 80 percent in the first year, plummeted to 36 percent in the 4th year, and further down to 10 percent in the 6th year. In Maine, it started as 100 percent in the first year, became 44 percent in the 2nd year, and dropped down to 6 percent in the 4th year. This implies that most schools would have enormous difficulty meeting the NCLB AYP requirement that appears to be an unrealistic expectation given a relatively high performance standard of proficiency and a relatively short time line (12 years).

Even when the rolling average option was used, it would have only slightly increased the chance of schools' meeting the AYP target (see Table 4.2). The chance of meeting AYP target with the rolling average was only 1.06 to 1.24 times greater than the chance of meeting AYP target without the rolling average. With the rolling averaging option, the percentage of schools that would meet their AYP target in the 2nd year, for example, may increase from 44.3 to 46 in Maine and from 35.9 to 39.5 in Kentucky. This implies that the rolling average has very weak potential to save schools from being identified as failing when their scores decline. Under NCLB, sanctions may apply to schools which fail to meet AYP for two or more consecutive years.

Many small elementary schools that tested only in one grade before NCLB (e.g., 4th) could double, triple or quadruple their effective sample size when third, fifth, and possible sixth grade (depending on the school configuration) results are included in AYP analyses under NCLB. The same can be said of middle schools that test only 8th grade now but may increase the sample size as many as four times once state assessments of grades 3–8 are put in place. If a school increases its effective testing sample size four times, it may reduce the school's standard error of AYP measure by up to one half.

It is particularly challenging to measure achievement for demographic subgroups in small, rural schools. Even in relatively large rural schools, the number of racial and ethnic minority students is likely to be much smaller than in typical urban schools. There are provisions to exempt states from the requirement to report or use disaggregated data when the number of students in a category is insufficient to yield statistically reliable information or the results would reveal personally identifiable information about an individual student. However, different states may develop different criteria about the minimum number of students to address this issue, since the U.S. Department of Education does not provide specific guidelines (MacQuarrie, 2002, September). While a higher minimum number yields fewer schools failing AYP, it has been shown that more valid and reliable AYP decisions can be made with a confidence interval, statistics-based, approach (Coladarci, 2003; Marion et al., 2002). However, it needs to be noted that the use of confidence intervals may reduce false positives but at the same time it will increase false negatives, that is, the chance that schools did not meet the standard but failed to be identified for improvement.

The current measure of school AYP is based on comparison of successive student groups' performance at the same grade level and tends to be highly unreliable (Kane & Staiger, 2002; Lee & Coladarci, 2002; Linn & Huag, 2002). This lack of reliability is more serious when the law requires reporting the progress of every major demographic subgroup in each school. Wrong identification of schools as needing academic improvement and the following misallocation of resources/aids may result from the use of unreliable AYP measures.

It has been argued that states should switch from this successive cohort model assessing different cohort groups' achievement to a longitudinal growth model assessing the same cohort's achievement gains (Wheat, 2000). For instance, schools may be evaluated by comparing this year's 3rd grade passing rates (i.e., percentage of students at or above Proficient level) with next year's 4th grade passing rates achieved by the same cohort of students. Currently the U.S. Department of Education is preparing to approve some states for this kind of growth-model pilot experiment (Hoff, 2006). Although this longitudinal evaluation method was shown to yield more reliable estimates of academic progress (Hill, 2001), it raises difficulties of the requirements that states must track individual students' academic performance over time and that performance standards must be comparable across adjacent grades. Further, as state and local education agencies are increasingly being held accountable for the education of highly mobile students, mobility rates of students could also limit a state's choice of this approach; longitudinal approaches would exclude large numbers of students in schools with high mobility (Marion et al., 2002; Paik & Phillips, 2002).

ARE SCHOOL ACCOUNTABILITY MEASURES FAIR?

Are current school accountability test measures fair? Fairness is an essential part of a comprehensive view of validity (Linn & Gronlund, 2000). Fairness of testing at the student level is whether all students have equal opportunities to learn what is tested and meet the performance standards. Fairness of accountability at the school or classroom level is whether all schools and teachers have equal capacity and resources to teach what is tested and have students meet the standards.

NCLB made one significant advancement in the treatment of fairness in school accountability by requiring disaggregation of performance by subgroups including minority and socioeconomically disadvantaged groups that should meet the same standards. It also avoids potential selection bias by requiring that almost all (95% or above) students in each subgroup participate in the assessment. However, this requirement makes relatively more diverse schools fall into the trap of being set to fail by virtue of demographic diversity. Studies show that schools that have more subgroups are less likely to make the AYP target (Kim & Sunderman, 2004). Since schools with more subgroups are not only more diverse but also more likely impoverished, the testing rule of subgroup disaggregation is not to blame for school failure; poverty can be a potential confounding factor of racial and ethnic diversity.

The U.S. Department of Education regulations do not permit calculating the starting points separately for any subgroups. By setting a uniform AYP target for every school and every student subgroup, the current formula does not consider the influence of schools' initial achievement status on their chance to meet the target consecutively. Higher-performing schools that are above the AYP target at the beginning will be able to meet the target much easier than lower-performing schools that are initially below the target. Even among those lower-performing schools, schools that are closer to the target initially are in a better position to meet the AYP target continuously. Figure 4.2 illustrates the problem. Suppose that there are two hypothetical schools and school A was initially performing above the statewide uniform AYP target (thick line applied uniformly to all schools) while school B was initially performing below the same target. Although both may ultimately reach the goal of 100% proficient in 12 years, they are likely to take quite different paths to the goal. If each of the two schools follows its projected linear performance trajectories (thin line applied separately to each school) as shown in Figure 4.2, school A would meet the target throughout the 12-year period, whereas school B would never meet the target until year 12. This result does not make sense because school B made much greater progress than school A throughout the period. In order to avoid becoming a failing school consecutively, school B would have to increase its performance substantially during the first year to reach its target. Nevertheless, this large initial increase in performance is very unlikely to happen, considering how much time and energy it might take to break through the natural tendency of incremental change and to fully implement new programs. If AYP targets are individualized following expected growth trajectories for each school, both school A and school B would be able to meet AYP targets more equally.

Does AYP measure school progress in a way that different groups of students in the same school can meet the same performance target at different rates? Basically, the law requires that schools disaggregate the test results into subgroups (e.g., major racial/ethnic groups, economically disadvantaged students, students with disabilities, English Language Learn-

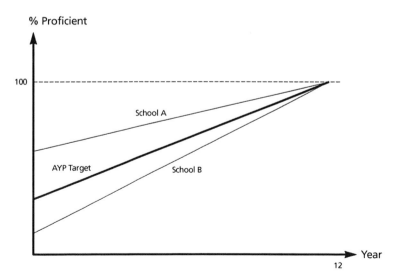

Figure 4.2.   Uniform AYP targets for all schools (thick line) vs. individualized AYP targets for two sample schools (thin lines), both aimed at the goal of 100% proficiency within 12-year timeline.

ers) and have all of them meet the same AYP target. While it is good to send the message that we want all groups of students to meet standards, this requirement has the danger of assuming that all categories will move forward at the same rates (NECEPL, 2002).

However, NCLB also gives schools the option of a "safe harbor", which is designed to lesson the difficulty of reaching the same AYP target for all groups of students at the same rates and give academically viable schools a second chance. For schools where the performance of one or more student subgroups on one or both of reading and math assessments fails to meet AYP targets, the school will be considered to have reached AYP under this provision if the percentage of students in that group who failed to reach proficiency decreased by 10 percent from the preceding year and also the group made progress on another academic indicator. However, previous research (Lee, 2004b) shows that this option is not powerful enough to avoid massive school failure under NCLB.

The current school accountability system in most states relies heavily on the indicators of schools' academic status rather their progress although they may combine the two pieces of information for final decision. However, the relationship between the status and progress of school achievement tends to be tenuous (Lee, 1998c; Raudenbush, 2004). School improvement levels are not strongly related to school performance levels: high performing schools do not necessarily improve more than low performing schools. A previous analysis of Maine schools' academic status vs. growth patterns (Lee, 1998c) identified factors that differentiate between the most and least improving schools as well as between the highest and lowest performing schools (see Figure 4.3 and 4.4). While the factors that show differences between the groups are quite similar between the school growth profile of Figure 4.3 and the school status profile of Figure 4.2, there are discrepancies in the size of group differences and the relative importance of family vs. school factors (see Appendix D for description of the variables). Particularly, the influence of school poverty becomes much less powerful in explaining the gap in growth than in status; the group difference in school poverty shrinks from 1.3 (Figure 4.2) to 0.7 (Figure 4.3) in a standard deviation unit. Raudenbush (2004) also shows that school accountability system using mean proficiency would disparately and unjustifiably identify high-poverty schools to be failing and that switching from the mean proficiency to the value-added approach would produce better results for high-poverty schools. However, it is noteworthy that the most improving schools still have better—albeit to a lesser degree—schooling conditions in terms of per pupil expenditures, teacher education and experience, and instructional resources than the least improving schools in Maine.

Raudenbush and Willms (1995) discuss two different types of school effects: Type A and Type B. Type A effect is the difference between a child's

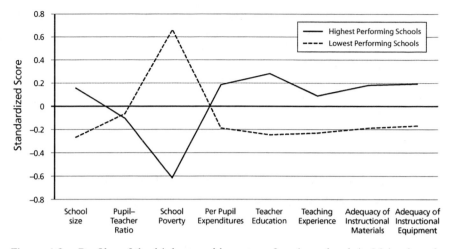

Figure 4.3.   Profiles of the highest and lowest performing schools in Maine based on 1990–97 MEA grade 4, 8, 11 reading and math assessment results.

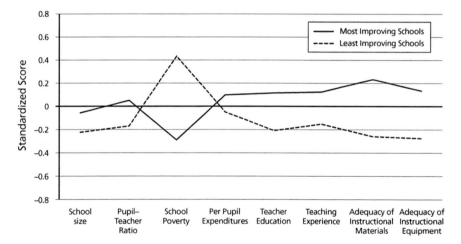

Figure 4.4.   Profiles of the most and least improving schools in Maine based on 1990–97 MEA grade 4, 8, 11 reading and math assessment results.

actual performance and the expected performance had that child attended a typical school. This effect doesn't concern whether that effectiveness derives from school inputs (e.g., class size, teacher quality) or from factors related to school context (e.g., community affluence, parental support). By contrast, a Type B effect isolates the effect of a school's input from any attending effects of school context. The two indicators are appropriate for purposes of school choice and school accountability, respectively (Meyer, 1997).[3]

Hierarchical linear modeling (HLM) is popular among educational researchers and evaluators for the estimation of value-added school effects (see Bryk, Thum, Easton, & Luppescu, 1998; Lee & Coladarci, 2002; Phillips & Adcock, 1997; Wainer, 2004; Yen, Schafer, & Rahman, 1999). HLM has been found to produce more stable school effect estimates than ordinary regression methods, particularly when schools have few students. Because public schools do not randomly assign students across schools and thus the estimation of school effects requires adequate statistical matching of student background characteristics, multilevel methods that afford decomposition of student-level and school-level variations became an attractive means for estimating school effects. HLM models also allow for considering the possibility that a school influences different groups of students differently (Raudenbush & Willms, 1995). Intuitively, a statistical model is fairer when it compares "like with like" by matching schools on (1) individual student-level family background factors and (2) school-level compositional effects out of schools' control.

However, the rationale for this statistical adjustment is counter to the logic of NCLB that all students can learn regardless of background. States have been resistant to such models due to the contradiction in the rationale of models and the underlying policy ideology of the law. Further, another concern may be that conducting such controls boils down to a normative, within-state comparison which might create cross-state variations and equity issues: how did school X with such and such a poverty level compare achievement wise with other schools in the state with similar poverty levels? This norm-referenced approach also is counter to the criterion-referenced tone of standards-based reform.

From even purely technical or scientific research perspective, this approach using statistical controls for school accountability can be challenged in a situation where there is systematic covariation between school context and school practice variables.[4] Conversely, one might argue that the differences among schools in school resources (including class size, teacher/administrator quality and instructional resources), possibly due to their different student demographic composition, are precisely what we need to remove for evaluating schools in fair ways. If high SES schools do a better job simply because they draw better staff, more resources, and better students, then this advantage should not be considered authentic "school" effects—i.e., differences among schools due to educational efforts and practices. Then, the task becomes to distinguish school inputs that are determined outside the school and sort out their effects as external school-level characteristics (Meyer, 1997). But this strategy can be problematic when the school input variables are highly correlated with school practice variables.

Even an accountability system based on value-added approach is vulnerable to criticisms that it will produce biased estimates of school effects on student learning (Raudenbush, 2004). Thus, the fundamental issue is not simply a technical choice of estimation methods. Rather, the estimation of school effects requires that we define "school effects" and formulate an explicit model of these effects (Raudenbush & Willms, 1995). In other words, this approach requires that the model be fully specified: All variables representing school input, practice, context, and student background would have to be measured and included in the model in order to guarantee that the effects of school practice were unbiased. Further, more qualitative information and expert judgment must be used in conjunction with such quantitative analysis of measures for triangulation.

ARE SCHOOL ACCOUNTABILITY MEASURES COMPREHENSIVE?

It is recommended that we use multiple measures if the measures are to be used for evaluation that will result in consequences for students and/or their school systems (see AERA, APA, & NCME, 1999). A one-shot state test alone is not sufficient to give reliable results or to cover all standards in sufficient depth. While most states rely exclusively on their own assessment for school accountability, there are serious concerns about using a single measure for such a high-stakes decision. Using more than a single measure may allow us to get a more comprehensive picture of student achievement and enhance the reliability and validity of evaluation.

NCLB demands multiple indicators (assessments of multiple subjects and inclusion of noncognitive indicators) and paves way to using multiple sources of assessment and multiple years of data. Here multiple, separate indicators refer to the measures of performance in multiple subjects including reading and mathematics plus another academic indicator (performance in other subject areas or attendance rate at the elementary level and graduation rate at the high school level).

However, using noncognitive indicators such as attendance, promotion, graduation and dropout rates for accountability has been criticized. First of all, many of these indicators have suffered from a lack of standardization in their computation (E. Baker, 2003). Moreover, these measures tend to show little variability or are substantially out of the control of schools (Koretz, 2003). Koretz points out that these measures may be more useful as a means of controlling inappropriate responses to high-stakes testing (e.g., increasing retention or dropout rates). Therefore, using these noncognitive measures alone should not be treated as meeting the requirement of multiple measures for accountability.

Under NCLB, states are allowed to use results from only statewide assessments, a combination of state and local assessments, or only local assessments for accountability purposes (Erpenbach et al., 2003). However, by making multiple sources of assessment an option, it does not require using more than one measure for an assessment of achievement in a single subject at a particular grade. Some see this option as a compromise that might result in assessment patchwork. States could use a combination of state and local assessments. States also could use either tests designed to assess students' achievement of state standards or tests designed to measure achievement against national norms. But if states did use what are called norm-referenced tests, they would have to alter them to fully reflect the states' standards. Use of commercial, off-the-shelf tests can bias effective learning goals away from the state's domain of curricular objectives. States that use such external tests not only will need to augment the tests with additional items for curricular areas that are unique to the state, but they also likely will need to remove some items that are outside their domains, fall at a different point in the sequence of learning, or are just simply markedly overemphasized if left in the state's AYP measures (Schafer, 2003). If states want to include locally-developed assessments in the state testing system, they also have to ensure that the assessments are aligned with state standards and are of acceptable technical quality.

States that are well-known for their use of locally-selected and/or locally-developed assessments, such as Maine, Nebraska, and Iowa, were approved under NCLB and had to make their cases for approval of accountability systems based on data derived from these assessments (Erpenbach et al., 2003). Justification for using local measures, particularly classroom assessment, is made on grounds of both fairness and validity. Classroom assessment can provide additional, rich opportunities for students to demonstrate their performance. Further, classroom assessments, administered over the full course of year, can provide more complete measures of the key standards identified by the state that are otherwise impractical to assess on a large-scale basis (Commission on Instructionally Supportive Assessment, 2001; E. Baker, 2003). A study of combining state and local assessment data from Maine schools suggests that the integrity of an achivement composite depends partly on the extent to which the component measures are drawing on the same universe of standards (Lee & Coladarci, 2002).

It is expected that local or state measures show considerably more growth than do more distal measures due to their better alignment with curriculum, instruction, and teacher professional development (E. Baker, 2003). In the same vein, local measures are likely to show inflation of achievement level and record more growth than are state measures. When states choose to use a combination of state and local assessments, state assessments could be used as a potential external validity criterion for local measures (E. Baker, 2003). Similar issues arise regarding the use of national and state assessment results for accountability and they are are examined in depth in Chapter 8, Part II.[5]

We need even broader definitions of multiple measures for accountability to take more systemic evaluation of whole school performance. Raudenbush (2004) contends that, despite their utility to parents and educators, current measures of school performance (either average proficiency score or value-added gain score) do not provide direct evidence of quality in school practice. Moreover, using more direct measures of educational practice for accountability can help reduce possible perverse incentives such as coaching and cheating in light of the threat of sanctions (see Koretz, 2003). While using proximate measures of achievement such as classroom assessment or using direct measures of educational practice may help avoid undesirable incentives of high-stakes testing, Koretz also notes that it is not realistically practical to incorporate these measures into a statewide accountability system and such an attempt would compromise measurement quality for improved incentives.

Despite potential problems and difficulties, using school input, practices, and contexts makes sense if the measures help us understand student outcomes. Many states tried to develop a more comprehensive educational database system to monitor and report on the quality of schooling. NCLB does not explicitly require states to have specific database structures, but it endorses databases that link students' test scores, enrollment, demographics, program participation, dropout, transfer and graduation records over time (Snow-Renner & Torrence, 2002). NCLB also requires state report cards include information on professional qualifications, the percentage of teachers with emergency or provisional credentials, and the percentage of classes not taught by highly qualified teachers, in aggregate and for schools in the top and bottom quartile of poverty in the state. According to the New England Center for Educational Policy and Leadership Tool Kit for Policymakers (p. 19),

> The shift in emphasis from inputs to results in accountability, which has taken place over the past few years, was certainly needed. But the march toward a results-based approach has neglected "opportunity to learn" indicators, which are critical inputs for explaining and changing the results. NCLB's call for data on professional qualifications opens a window on OTL and might add legitimacy to the OTL indicators.

However, measures of schooling conditions and resources tend to be missing in the school report card. Among the 36 states that reported having an annual report card on each of its schools as of 1999, only half provided information on teachers, resources, and school climate ("Quality

Counts '99", 1999). Moreover, racial and socioeconomic disparities among schools in key resources were not reported. This implies that the adequacy and equality of educational resources and opportunities were not considered in evaluating school performance for accountability. Because NCLB requires reporting disaggregated achievement data by racial and socioeconomic subgroups, it is equally critical to do the same for schooling resources.

CONCLUSION

It is important to remember that tests or their results in themselves are not necessarily valid or invalid. What matters in validation is the interpretation, use and impact of test results. Do we interpret and use the test results in appropriate ways? Do those interpretations and uses have desirable consequences for teaching and learning? In a similar vein, an accountability system that used test results as performance indicators for rewards/sanctions, in themselves, are neither valid nor invalid. What matters are the ultimate decisions based on the measures in this accountability system, decisions that have consequences for the targets of accountability.

The most imminent challenge of measuring AYP is the threat of misidentifying failing schools and attributing their failure to wrong reasons. NCLB identifies schools needing improvement each year primarily based on the status of student achievement rather than progress, except that the safe harbor option considers progress when schools fail to meet the target only for subgroups. If the formula ignores disparities among schools in starting points, demographics, resources and capacity, it will unduly identify and penalize disadvantaged minority schools. This false identification and attribution may threaten the validity of NCLB accountability policy.

Since poor, high-minority schools have a greater risk of failing to meet state-imposed, uniform AYP targets, it may not be very fair to apply the same criteria of evaluation to all schools across the nation and states in the same ways. While the individualized AYP-setting approach with different starting points for different schools may help identify schools in need of real improvement, efforts to make causal attributions of test results to schools remain problematic. Further, the new approach implies changes in the current law and raises controversies about the underlying premise of the law that schools must have all students meet the same standards regardless of background. In order to address this issue within the parameters of the current law and regulations, states still need to fully assess the unique needs of disadvantaged low-performing schools and provide them with special means to an end that is more equitable.

NOTES

1. These estimates of correlations between NAEP and state assessment scores may have been attenuated due to the restriction of range in school-level aggregate scores; the standard deviation of school average math scores was less than half of the standard deviation of individual students' math scores. Thus, the above correlation coefficients have been corrected for restricted ranges: .79 (grade 4) and .82 (grade 8) in Kentucky and .89 (grade 4) and .91 (grade 8) in Maine.

2. Despite considerable agreement at the level of broad content area and basic organization of math, NAEP and state assessments may reveal differences at the item level in operationalization of content and item format. According to an Education Week report, states have trouble meeting a requirement to provide performance descriptors that students must master in specific content areas at a specific grade level to reach a particular performance level, such as "proficiency" (Olson, 2005b).

3. There have been real-world attempts to sort out school effects for accountability purposes (i.e., Type B effect) through comparison of each school's or teacher's performance over time while controlling for the characteristics of schools and teachers. One well-known example of this longitudinal accountability model is Tennessee's Value-Added Assessment System (TVAAS) (Sanders, Saxton, & Horn, 1997). This system tests students in grades 2 through 8 to keep track of achievement gains from year to year and compare them with gains made by a normative sample. The data are used to evaluate "value added" by a teacher or by a school. (A legislative review of the TVAAS is available at http://www.comptroller.state.tn.us/orea/reports/tvaas.pdf). Raudenbush and Willms (1995, p. 332) point out the problem of causal inference: "Causal inference is much more problematic in the case of Type B effects because the treatment—school practice—is typically undefined so that the correlation between school context and school practice cannot be computed. Thus, even if the assignment of students to schools were strongly ignorable, the assignment of schools to treatments could not be."

4. Bryk and Raudenbush (1992, p. 127–128) explains the problem where there exist differences in school staff quality that might confound the effects of school staff with the effects of student composition:

    > Suppose that the Group 2 schools [schools having similarly high social-class composition] have more effective staff and that staff quality, not student composition, causes the elevated test scores. The results could occur, for example, if the school district assigned its best principals and teachers to the more affluent schools. If so, the second strategy [statistical adjustment for compositional effects] would give no credit to these leaders for their effective practices.

5. Lee (in press) examined discrepencies between NAEP and state assessments in Kentucky and Maine regarding three indicators of state performance: proficiency level, achievement gap, and achievement gain. The study suggests that the testing gap is attributable to multiple factors, including standard-setting methods, test design, and testing environment.

PART II

IMPACT OF NCLB AND STATE ACCOUNTABILITY ON THE ACHIEVEMENT GAP

CHAPTER 5

SHATTERED VISIONS OF NCLB AND STATE ACCOUNTABILITY

MIXED REACTIONS TO POST-NCLB NAEP READING AND MATH ACHIEVEMENT TRENDS

NAEP can provide timely information to states regarding their students' achievement against high performance standards in core subject areas. In light of the controversies about the impact of NCLB on student outcomes, many people were anxious to see the NAEP 2005 results, which reported the national and state average reading and math performance from testing nationally representative samples of more than 300,000 4th and 8th graders (Perie, Grigg, & Donahue, 2005a for reading; Perie, Grigg, & Dion, 2005b for math). Since the U.S. Department of Education released the NAEP 2005 reports on October 19, 2005, reactions to these reports varied. The U.S. Department of Education newsletter, *The Achiever* (Vol. 4 No. 12, Nov/Dec 2005), noted, "overall math scores for both groups (4th and 8th graders) rose to all-time highs, and fourth-grade reading scores matched the all-time record." The U.S. Secretary of Education attributed credit for such gains to NCLB, who claimed "These results, like the long-term July data, confirm that we are on the right track with No Child Left Behind, particularly with younger students who have benefited from the core principles of annual assessment and disaggregation of data." (*The Achiever*, p. 2). Critics of standardized testing interpreted the 2005 NAEP results more negatively. The National Center for Fair and Open Testing (FairTest, 2005, October 19) commented on the NAEP 2005 report in its press release: "Flatline NAEP scores show the failure of test-driven school reform. No

The Testing Gap, pages 87–69

Child Left Behind has not improved academic performance." FairTest claimed that "NAEP reading scores were essentially unchanged from 2002 to 2005 at grade 4 and declined markedly at grade 8." FairTest also pointed out that "math scores did not increase at a significantly faster rate than in the 1990s, well before most high-stakes exams for elementary and middle school were put in place."

The different interpretations of the same results may be attributed partly to differences in the time frame used to analyze changes in the test results and different ways of evaluating the policy impact. To understand whether short-term improvements in NAEP scores can be attributed to NCLB, we need to assess any short-term changes in scores within a longer-term time frame. This will allow us to determine whether NCLB had a significant effect on academic growth or if the changes were the continuation of a growth pattern that began before NCLB and continued after its passage. In addition, changes in NAEP scores need to be analyzed within the broader context of testing and accountability policy.

DISCREPANCIES BETWEEN NAEP AND STATES' ASSESSMENT REPORTS ON READING AND MATH ACHIEVEMENT TRENDS

State assessments are the basis for states' educational accountability decision-making under NCLB. Although NCLB does not prescribe a role for NAEP in making state accountability decisions, it does specify using NAEP scores to confirm state test results, to evaluate the rigor of state standards, and to show whether states are making progress in improving student achievement and reducing the achievement gap among concerned subgroups of students (Ad Hoc Committee on Confirming Test Results, 2002; Henderson-Montero, Julian, & Yen, 2003). Previous comparisons of NAEP and state assessment results showed significant discrepancies in the level of student achievement, as well as in the size of statewide achievement gains (Fuller et al., 2006; Klein et al., 2000; Koretz & Barron, 1998; Lee, in press; Linn et al., 2002). The percentages of students reaching the Proficient level tend to be generally lower on NAEP than on state assessments. These results suggest that, for many states, NAEP proficiency levels are more challenging than the states' own (National Education Goals Panel, 1996). Further, statewide gains in proficiency rate tend to be larger on state assessments than on NAEP. Since state standards vary widely in relationship to NAEP standards, it raises questions about the generalizability of gains reported on a state's own assessment, and hence about the validity of claims regarding student achievement (Linn, 2000).

While several studies have attempted to examine the impact of NCLB on student achievement, they are limited because they use a single measure of achievement only "after" NCLB was adopted. Any change we see after NCLB may reflect a continuing trend that occurred before NCLB. Any changes that were clearly on track before NCLB should not be credited to the new law. While it is important to maintain the pace of improvement, it is inappropriate to credit NCLB for improving achievement if the law did not accelerate the pace. States tend to show progress on their own standards regardless of whether or not it transfers into progress independently measured by NAEP. For example, a report by the Education Trust (2004) on post-NCLB achievement trends relied solely on states' own assessment results. The report examined short-term changes in average achievement in state reading and math assessment results and changes in racial and economic achievement gaps after NCLB (from 2002 to 2004). The findings of this report suggest that the improvements in performance were positive but that narrowing the gap was slow. A follow-up report by the Education Trust (2006) takes a more comprehensive look into post-NCLB changes across grade levels (from 2003 to 2005) and finds more positive results at the elementary education level than at the secondary level. According to a report by the Center on Education Policy (2006), national survey results show that scores on state tests have risen in a large majority of states and school districts. That report credited school district policies and programs as more important contributors to these gains than the NCLB AYP requirements. Despite these earlier findings, real full-scale impact of NCLB on student achievement remains to be examined.

DESIGN AND ORGANIZATION OF STUDIES IN PART II

Part II offers a systematic analysis of trends on national and state-level public school students' reading and math achievement using data from NAEP (see Appendix E for descriptions of data and methods). Particular attention is paid to the achievement gap among racial and socioeconomic groups of students.[1] In this study, racial achievement gaps focus on the gaps between Blacks and Whites and between Hispanics and Whites. Socioeconomic achievement gap is measured by the gap between Poor (those eligible for free or reduced-priced school lunch) and Nonpoor student groups. National and state progress toward closing achievement gaps are evaluated not only in terms of their success in reducing the achievement gap in test scores but also in terms of reducing each subgroup's chance of failing to meet desired performance standards.

Chapter 6 reports findings from trend analyses that explore the effects of NCLB accountability policy on student achievement outcomes. Trend analyses involves fitting statistical models with estimates of pre-NCLB and post-NCLB change parameters based on a series of measurements on key outcome criteria obtained at periodic intervals before and after NCLB. It enables the evaluator to interpret the pre-to-post-NCLB changes by showing whether the achievement gains after NCLB are a continuation of earlier trends or whether they mark a decisive change. It is important to look at both average scores over time and trends in the achievement gap, since narrowing the gap without improving average scores is not progress. Particularly, this study compares the Pre-NCLB Period (1990–2001) with the Post-NCLB Period (2002–2005).[2]

Figure 5.1 illustrates three potential growth patterns that may result from NCLB policies. When NCLB has a significant positive effect, the performance trajectory will shift upwards with a marked increase in the growth rate (Scenario A in Figure 5.1). In this case, we expect sustained positive gain after NCLB so that post-NCLB growth rate is significantly greater than pre-NCLB growth rate. When NCLB has a significant negative effect, the performance trajectory will shift downwards with a marked decrease in the growth rate (Scenario C in Figure 5.1). When NCLB has no effect at all, a preexisting growth pattern will continue (Scenario B in Figure 5.1). In this case, we expect no change in the slope so that pre-NCLB and post-NCLB growth rates remain the same.

If the analysis were to find a distinctive effect of NCLB, it could not, of course, be attributed to just one part of NCLB such as high-stakes testing and school accountability. Other policy initiatives under NCLB, such as teacher qualification and parental involvement policies, and an initial

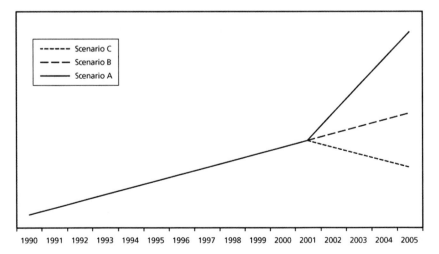

Figure 5.1.   Hypothetical Achievement Trends Before and After NCLB: Positive Effect (Scenario A), No Effect (Scenario B), Negative Effect (Scenario C).

influx of new federal funds, may have influenced the trends as well.[3] It is not possible to sort out the effect of one particular policy component from such an omnibus legislation. Moreover, some states that had high-stakes testing accountability prior to NCLB continued their own policies along with NCLB, thus creating a dual accountability system. By the same token, the pre-NCLB period is not free of similar types of interventions since some of the states already had their own accountability systems in place.

In Chapter 7, the study addresses variation among states in NAEP growth rates by taking into account their accountability policy history prior to NCLB. States which did not have high-stakes accountability policies before NCLB and were only exposed to the influences of external accountability under NCLB are compared with states that were active in test-driven accountability policy prior to NCLB. This analysis compares differences in both pre-NCLB and post-NCLB growth rates between two groups of states. States that adopted accountability polices before NCLB are called "first-generation" accountability states and include Kentucky, Maryland, North Carolina, California, Florida, New York, and Texas (Mintrop & Trujillo, 2005). States that never initiated statewide accountability reform before NCLB are called "second-generation" accountability states for the sake of distinction, whether they embraced NCLB or not.

Lawmakers did not intend that NCLB would replace a state's preexisting accountability policy where a parallel system already existed but rather would function as an add-on to enhance or augment state policy.[4] States with strong accountability systems may be better prepared to embrace and implement NCLB reform policy since implementation theory predicts stronger implementation fidelity among people who are accustomed to the intervention. No matter what real impact NCLB may have had on first generation states, the primary target of NCLB may have been second-generation states—those states where test-driven external accountability was new and where NCLB attempted to extend accountability modeled after the alleged success stories of some first-generation states such as Texas and North Carolina. By this logic, states with no exposure to high-stakes testing prior to NCLB are more likely to experience the effect of this new intervention by accelerating the pre-NCLB growth rate.

Hierarchical linear modeling (HLM) method, growth curve modeling, was used to examine trends in achievement in first and second generation states, recognizing that comparing two nonequivalent groups poses a threat to the validity of causal inferences about NCLB. The initial performance status gap (i.e., test score difference in 1990) reflects the fact that lower-achieving states were more active in adopting test-driven external accountability policies prior to NCLB. Until NCLB, states adopting test-driven accountability systems (first generation states) were expected to make greater test score gains than states not adopting these types of reforms (second generation states). After NCLB, both were likely to make about the same rate of growth. Consequently, second generation states may make greater pre- to post-NCLB progress in test score gains than their first generation counterparts. Latent variable HLM analysis was used to control for the effect of initial status on pre-NCLB gain and also the effect of pre-NCLB growth rate on post-NCLB change.

In Chapter 8, the study examines discrepancies between NAEP and states' own assessment results, explores factors, such as the degree of high-stakes testing, that might account for variations among states in these patterns, and discusses the policy implications of these findings. Previous studies that compared state assessments with NAEP scores were often restricted to a single state and did not systematically examine patterns across multiple grades and subjects from all states. In particular, those prior studies did not often look into possible differences between NAEP and state assessments in their estimation of the achievement gaps, an important indicator of state performance in educational equity (for exceptions, Lee, in press; Linton & Kester, 2003).

In light of these concerns, we need to examine whether and how both NAEP scores and states' own student assessments can be used to inform us of statewide academic performance. We also need to examine whether national and state assessments produce consistent results over time, particularly before and after NCLB. This requires a systematic comparative analysis of national and state student assessment data, specifically data on the proficiency levels of students, the achievement gaps among different racial groups of students, and their academic progress. The objective of the analysis presented in Chapter 8 is to investigate discrepancies between national and state assessment results at the state level and to explain interstate variations in the discrepancies.

One should interpret the findings from this study cautiously. This evaluation of the impact of NCLB on improving student achievement and narrowing the achievement gaps uses currently available NAEP data. Analysis over a longer time period may produce different results. Since there are only a few years of NAEP or state assessment data available for post-NCLB analysis, it may be premature to evaluate the full impact of NCLB as the policy sets 2014 as the deadline for states to meet it performance targets. Secondly, this analysis of repeated cross-sectional data confounds the policy effect and the cohort effect.[5] To address the possible influence of the cohort effect, we would also need to analyze demographic changes (racial and economic composition of successive cohort groups), something that requires long-term data.

With these caveats in mind, the findings of this study still have implications for NCLB, and test-driven external accountability policy in particular, as we approach the debate about reauthorization. Findings from the following series of extensive statistical data analyses are expected to provide policymakers and practitioners with useful information on the national and state trends in achievement gaps and can be used to help them develop policies that improve both equity and excellence. This study is also expected to inform policymakers of the discrepancies between NAEP and states' own assessment results and the importance of using multiple measures for accountability.

NOTES

1. This study does not include students with disabilities (SWD) and English Language Learners (ELL) primarily due to concerns about their relatively small sample size and reliability of estimates. It never implies that the achievement gap of these or other subgroups excluded from the study do not count for equity.

2. Although the national achievement trends are simply divided into the two time periods, that is, pre-NCLB (1990–2001) vs. post-NCLB (2002–2005) for the sake of analysis, the pre-NCLB trend may reflect the influence of a precursor to NCLB, the Improving America's School Act (IASA) of 1994. It needs to be noted that IASA required states to develop assessment systems for measuring AYP, but NCLB substantially strengthened the scope and intensity of test-driven external accountability provisions by targeting all schools as opposed to Title 1 schools only as well as imposing more stringent requirements (e.g., meeting AYP for all subgroups) with real threats of punitive and corrective actions.

3. For the theory of action for educational accountability policy, see Adams and Kirst (1999), Elmore and Fuhrman (1995), Fuhrman (1999), Lee and Wong (2004), Newmann et al. (1997), O'Day (2002).

4. The existence of dual accountability systems and interactions between federal and state policies under NCLB poses methodological challenges for the analysis of post-NCLB data. Hanushek and Raymond (2004) point out the problem in that the implementation of NCLB essentially precludes analysis of further impacts of overall accountability systems by eliminating comparison group of states without accountability systems but at the same time the possibility that the continuation of individual states' own locally developed schemes affords comparison of the impacts of alternative types of accountability systems. NCLB also provides funding to support school improvement programs, and the interaction between NCLB accountability policy and preexisting school reform strategies such as Comprehensive School Reform (CSR) may affect the policy impact (LeFloch, Taylor, & Thomsen, 2006).

5. Concern about the cohort effect arises from the possibility that changes in the demographic compositions of NAEP student samples coincide with the policy intervention and both policy and demographic forces influence achievement trends at the same time (see Appendix E).

CHAPTER 6

NATIONAL ACHIEVEMENT
TRENDS IN NAEP

Using NAEP reading and math assessment data from 1990 to 2005, the following analysis examines national trends in 4th and 8th grade students' academic growth before and after NCLB. The first section uses scale scores, that is, scores that summarizes the overall performance attained by a group of students on the NAEP, to show how average reading and math scores have changed over time. The second section examines changes in the percentage of students reaching the NAEP proficiency level, that is, the percentage of students, either in the total population or in a subgroup, that meet or exceed the NAEP proficiency level.[1]

NATIONAL NAEP READING
AND MATH SCALE SCORE TRENDS

Trends in the Average Achievement: Trends in national average reading and math gains on the NAEP are shown in Figure 6.1 and 6.2 respectively.[2] When comparing the average gains in reading achievement scores before NCLB with gains made after NCLB, we find no differences in the amount of gains made in grade 4 reading scores (Figure 6.1). Reading scores did not improve after NCLB and made only modest improvements prior to NCLB. In grade 8, there was a marked decline in average reading scores after NCLB compared to the pre-NCLB period. In contrast, math achievement scores showed significant improvement both before and after NCLB

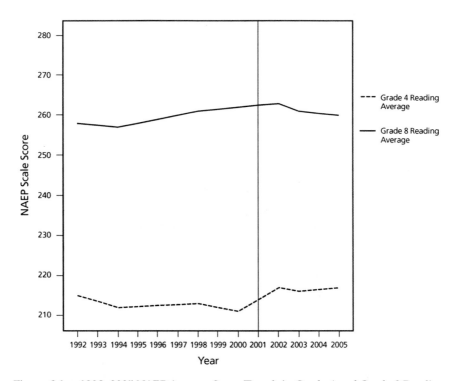

Figure 6.1.   1992–2005 NAEP Average Score Trends in Grade 4 and Grade 8 Reading

in both grades (Figure 6.2). However, the post-NCLB achievement growth pattern was not different from the pre-NCLB growth patterns.

In order to test for the statistical significance of the trends described above for each subject and grade, time-series regression analyses of national NAEP public school students' 1992–2005 reading and 1990–2005 math scale scores were conducted. The results are summarized in Table 6.1 for reading and in Table 6.2 for math; both pre-NCLB and post-NCLB growth patterns for each subgroup are classified by the significance and direction of changes. The pre-NCLB growth dimension (rows in the Tables 6.1 and 6.2) tells how the outcome measures for each group changed before NCLB: up (significantly upward trend), down (significantly downward trend); flat (no significant trend). The post-NCLB change dimension (columns in the Tables 6.1 and 6.2) tells how the pre-NCLB growth pattern changed after NCLB: increment (significant post-NCLB gain); decrement (significant post-NCLB loss); same (no significant change).

In contrast with trends in math, the national trend in NAEP reading achievement has followed more mixed growth patterns through the 1992–2005 period (see Table 6.1). As already shown by graphs, the average reading achievement trend tends to be flatter than the average math

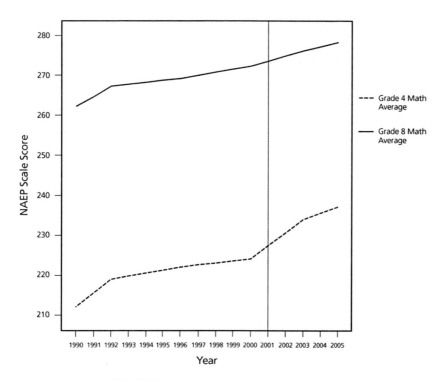

Figure 6.2.   1990–2005 NAEP Average Score Trends in Grade 4 and Grade 8 Math.

achievement trend. For grade 4, there was no significant improvement at all throughout the entire period. None of the pre-NCLB growth and post-NCLB change estimates in reading (except for pre-NCLB growth among Asians) are significant. For grade 8, the average reading score improved significantly during the pre-NCLB period, but this gain has dropped after NCLB, signifying some setback in national reading progress. The pre-NCLB growth estimates in reading are significantly positive, whereas the post-NCLB change estimates are significantly negative.

As shown in Table 6.2, the results of NAEP 4th and 8th grade math trend analysis show that the national average level of NAEP math achievement improved significantly throughout the pre-NCLB period in math (except for a few subgroups). As shown by the "Pre-NCLB Growth" rows of Table 6.2, the national average math achievement tended to improve significantly. However, comparison of the growth rates between the pre-NCLB period and the post-NCLB period reveals that there was no change in the rate of growth after NCLB. As shown by the "Post-NCLB Change" columns of Table 6.2, none of them are significant. While the average math score continued to rise and reached an all time record high in 2005, there is no indication that the improvement of average math scores accelerated after

TABLE 6.1
National Pre-NCLB and Post-NCLB Trends in NAEP Grade 4 and Grade 8 Reading Achievement by Subgroups

| | | Post-NCLB Change | | |
		Increment	Same	Decrement
	Up		Hispanic (8), Asian (4)	All (8), White (8), Black (8), Nonpoor (8)
Pre-NCLB Growth	Flat		All (4), White (4), Black (4), Hispanic (4), Asian (8), Nonpoor (4), Poor	
	Down			

Note. Numbers in parenthesis refer to grades in which different growth patterns are observed. When the same growth patterns apply to both grades 4 and 8 in each subgroup or gap, no numbers are shown after the group or gap name. For the "all" and each subgroup categories, "up" means improvement of the average, whereas "down" means decline of the average.

TABLE 6.2
National Pre-NCLB and Post-NCLB Trends in NAEP Grade 4 and Grade 8 Math Achievement by Subgroups

| | | Post-NCLB Change | | |
		Increment	Same	Decrement
	Up	Hispanic (8)	All, White, Black	
Pre-NCLB Growth	Flat		Hispanic (4), Asian, Nonpoor, Poor,	
	Down			

Note. Numbers in parenthesis refer to grades in which different growth patterns are observed. When the same growth patterns apply to both grades 4 and 8 in each subgroup or gap, no numbers are shown after the group or gap name. For the "all" and each subgroup categories, "up" means improvement of the average, whereas "down" means decline of the average.

NCLB across the board. The only exception to this general pattern is Hispanic 8th grade, which appears to have gained further after NCLB.

Trends in the Achievement Gap:　The racial achievement gap persists after NCLB. The achievement gap between White and Black students and between White and Hispanic students remained unchanged in both reading and math in both grades 4 and 8. The only significant change was a small reduction in the achievement gap between White and Hispanic students in grade 8 math. Likewise, the gap between Poor and Nonpoor students remained.

Figure 6.3 and Figure 6.4 show the NAEP trends in the White–Black achievement gap between 1992 and 2005 in reading and between 1990 and 2005 for math. Although there was a temporary drop between 2000 and 2003 in the grade 8 math White–Black gap, the gap leveled off afterwards. There was more progress in reducing the Black–White gap in math for fourth graders. However, the pattern of post-NCLB change in the gap was not significantly different from its corresponding pre-NCLB trend.

Similarly, Hispanic–White reading and math achievement gaps have hardly changed over the period. Figure 6.5 and Figure 6.6 show the NAEP trends in the White-Hispanic achievement gap between 1992 and 2005 in reading and between 1990 and 2005 for math. Although there was a temporary drop between 2000 and 2003 in the grade 4 math White-Hispanic gap, the gap leveled off afterwards. A similar pattern is found in grade 4 reading. Consequently, the White-Hispanic gap in reading and math has returned back to its baseline level by 2005.

As shown in Figure 6.7 and Figure 6.8, the poverty gap also did not change significantly in both reading and math at grades 4 and 8. The post-NCLB trend was not different from the pre-NCLB trend, which also showed no significant changes in the gap.

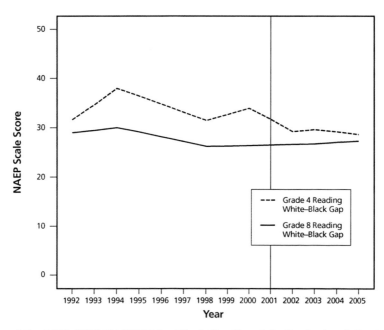

Figure 6.3.   1992–2005 NAEP White–Black Gap Trends in Grade 4 and Grade 8 Reading.

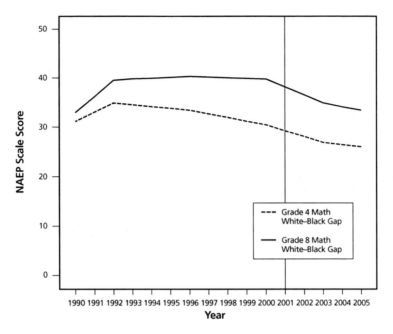

Figure 6.4.   1990–2005 NAEP White–Black Gap Trends in Grade 4 and Grade 8 Math.

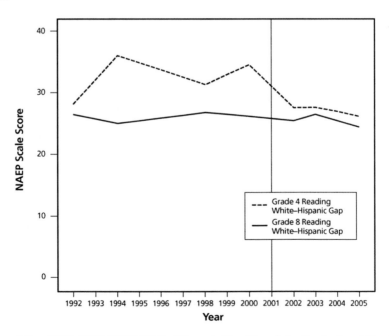

Figure 6.5.   1992–2005 NAEP White-Hispanic Gap Trends in Grade 4 and Grade 8 Reading.

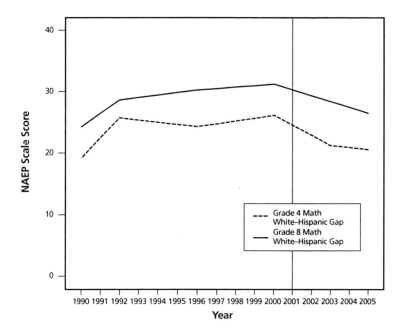

Figure 6.6.   1990–2005 NAEP White-Hispanic Gap Trends in Grade 4 and Grade 8 Math.

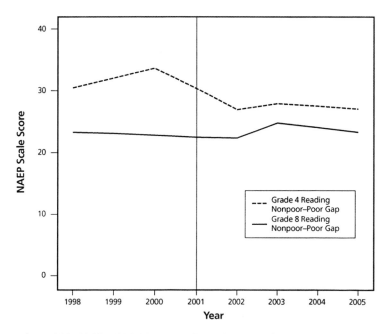

Figure 6.7.   1998–2005 NAEP Nonpoor-Poor Gap Trends in Grade 4 and Grade 8 Reading.

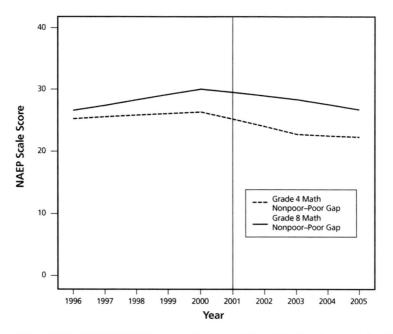

Figure 6.8.   1996–2005 NAEP Nonpoor-Poor Gap Trends in Grade 4 and Grade 8 Math.

In order to test for the statistical significance of the trends described above for each subject and grade, time-series regression analyses of national NAEP public school students' 1992–2005 reading and 1990–2005 math scale score gaps were conducted. The results are summarized in Table 6.3 for reading and in Table 6.4 for math; both pre-NCLB and post-NCLB growth patterns for achievement gaps are classified by the significance and direction of changes.

The gaps among racial and socioeconomic groups in both grade 4 and grade 8 reading remained the same, and there were no significant changes in the gaps before or after NCLB (Table 6.3). Racial and socioeconomic achievement gaps in math also remained the same throughout the 1990–2005 period (Table 6.4). This suggests that all subgroups made about the same amount of achievement gains after NCLB as they did before, and that the achievement gaps did not narrow or widen significantly following the implementation of NCLB. The only exception to this general pattern is the White-Hispanic 8th grade math gap, which narrowed significantly after NCLB.

TABLE 6.3
National Pre-NCLB and Post-NCLB Trends in NAEP Grade 4 and Grade 8 Reading Achievement by Subgroups and their Gaps

| | | Post-NCLB Change | | |
		Increment	Same	Decrement
Pre-NCLB Growth	Up			
	Flat		White–Black gap, White-Hispanic gap, Poverty gap	
	Down			

Note. Numbers in parenthesis refer to grades in which different growth patterns are observed. When the same growth patterns apply to both grades 4 and 8 in each subgroup or gap, no numbers are shown after the group or gap name. For the racial and poverty gaps, "up" signifies widening of the gap, whereas "down" signifies narrowing of the gap.

TABLE 6.4
National Pre-NCLB and Post-NCLB Trends in NAEP Grade 4 and Grade 8 Math Achievement by Subgroups and their Gaps

| | | Post-NCLB Change | | |
		Increment	Same	Decrement
Pre-NCLB Growth	Up			
	Flat		White–Black gap, White-Hispanic gap (4), Poverty gap	White-Hispanic gap (8)
	Down			

Note. Numbers in parenthesis refer to grades in which different growth patterns are observed. When the same growth patterns apply to both grades 4 and 8 in each subgroup or gap, no numbers are shown after the group or gap name. For the racial and poverty gaps, "up" signifies widening of the gap, whereas "down" signifies narrowing of the gap.

NATIONAL NAEP READING
AND MATH PROFICIENCY TRENDS

Trends in the Average Proficiency: In this section, the percent of students scoring at or above the proficient level on the NAEP are examined and the pre-NCLB trends in proficiency are compared to the post-NCLB trends. NAEP proficiency levels instead of scale scores are used. This trend analysis focuses on the percentage of students meeting or exceeding the desired NAEP performance standard, that is, students performing at or above the "Proficient" level.

The percentage of students nationally scoring at or above proficient on the NAEP in reading and math did not change significantly after NCLB (Figures 6.9 and 6.10). If we assume that the nation stays on the current trajectory, the results of trend analysis project that by 2014 only 24 to 34 percent of students would meet the reading proficiency target and about 29–64 percent of students would meet the math proficiency target.[3]

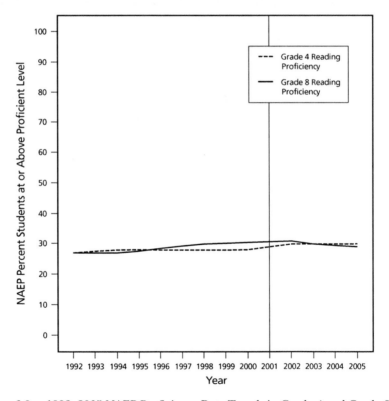

Figure 6.9.   1992–2005 NAEP Proficiency Rate Trends in Grade 4 and Grade 8 Reading.

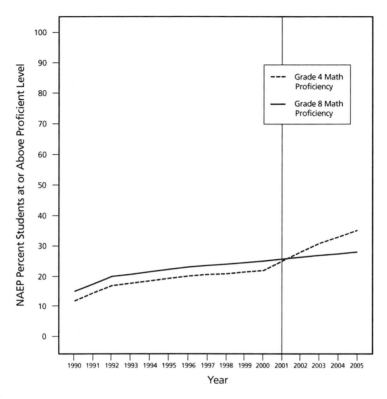

Figure 6.10.   1990–2005 NAEP Proficiency Rate Trends in Grade 4 and Grade 8 Math.

Trends in the Proficiency Gap: If current trends in the racial and socioeconomic achievement gaps continue, substantial disparities in proficiency rates between advantaged White and disadvantaged minority groups will persist. Under the assumption that the current trajectories will continue, it is projected that by 2014 between 32 and 44 percent of Whites will reach the reading proficiency target and 40–78 percent will reach the math proficiency target. In contrast, 7 to 18 percent of Blacks will achieve proficiency in reading and 25–55 percent in math. Among Hispanics, 14 to 21 percent will achieve proficiency in reading and 32–70 percent will achieve proficiency in math. Thirty-two to thirty-eight percent of Nonpoor students will achieve proficiency in reading and 47–81 percent will reach proficiency in math, whereas only 11–16 percent of Poor students will achieve proficiency in reading and 20–76 percent in math. Obviously the feasibility of reaching the proposed goal of 100 percent proficiency raises serious concerns, particularly for disadvantaged minority students and their schools.

There was a period when the racial achievement gap narrowed substantially with significant academic progress of Blacks and Hispanics. Prior research based on the long-term trend NAEP showed that the racial achievement gaps narrowed at the basic skills level in the 1970s and early 1980s but grew at the advanced skills level in the late 1980s and the 1990s (Lee, 2002). Even if there were significant reductions of the achievement gaps in certain areas after NCLB, they may be viewed as relatively much small when compared to the magnitude of the past decreases. The overall Black–White and Hispanic–White achievement gaps remained substantially large at the high achievement level that current NAEP proficiency standard signifies.

CONCLUSION

The goal of NCLB, which requires that states have all students accomplish high standards of learning in core subject areas (i.e., 100% of students become proficient in reading and math by 2014), is laudable. Past and current NAEP reading and math achievement trends, however, raise serious concerns about the unrealistic performance goal and timeline and the possible consequences for schools that repeatedly fail to meet their performance target. If the nation continues to make the same amount of achievement gains as it did over the past 15 years, it may end up meeting only less than half of the reading proficiency target and less than two-thirds of the math proficiency target by 2014. These projections become much gloomier when it comes to closing the achievement gaps for disadvantaged minority students who are even more left behind in reading and math proficiency. However, it is worth noting that enormous progress was made in narrowing racial achievement gaps in the 1970s and 1980s (e.g., reduction of the Black–White math gap by half). This implies that further progress in closing the gap can be made through social and educational policies, reversing the setback in the 1990s.

In order to find out whether test-driven external accountability policy, the hallmark of NCLB, works, we need to know how well the nation and states have accomplished the goals of academic excellence and equity before NCLB as well as after NCLB. What do we learn from comparisons of pre-NCLB vs. post-NCLB NAEP trends of reading and math achievement? The results of national NAEP trend analyses suggest that NCLB did not have significant impact on improving reading and math achievement across the nation and states so far. The national average achievement remains flat in reading and grows at the same pace in math after NCLB that it did prior to NCLB. It is misleading to claim that NCLB has a positive effect on academic achievement simply because the national average math test scores continue to rise after NCLB. This inference is flawed because the increase in NAEP scores was just part of trend that began before NCLB and does not reflect any significant acceleration in the pace of academic improvement after NCLB. Nevertheless, it can also be misleading to discredit any potential effects of NCLB on achievement gains in the future by simply looking at the overall national growth trend in such a relatively short time period. Since some states had implemented their own school accountability systems long before NCLB, the impact of NCLB on individual states may be uneven or obscured by looking at the national aggregate picture. Interstate variations in accountability policies and student outcomes are examined in the next chapter.

NOTES

1. There are three achievement levels on the NAEP: Basic, Proficient, and Advanced. The achievement levels were authorized by the NAEP legislation and adopted by the National Assessment Governing Board (NAGB). They are collective judgments, gathered from a broadly representative panel of teachers, education specialists, and members of the general public, about what students should know and be able to do relative to a body of content reflected in the NAEP assessment frameworks. For reporting purposes, the achievement level cut scores for each grade are placed on the traditional NAEP scale resulting in four ranges: below Basic, Basic, Proficient, and Advanced. For example, the Proficient level of 8th grade math achievement was set at a score of 299 on a 0 to 500 NAEP scale, and eighth-grade students performing at this level should exhibit evidence of conceptual and procedural understanding in math (Mullis et al., 1993).

2. NAEP results with accommodation permitted are shown for 1998–2005 years in reading and for 1996–2005 years in math. All prior assessments were done without accommodation.

3. Since these projections are based on the results of both grade 4 and grade 8 samples and there are often divergence of the trends between the two grades (e.g., faster growth in grade 4 than in grade 8 in math), a relatively wide range of estimates is given.

CHAPTER 7

STATE ACHIEVEMENT TRENDS IN NAEP

Notwithstanding the aggregate national NAEP trends, there are substantial variations among states in growth patterns on the NAEP state assessment. This chapter examines changes in individual state performance in reading and math using data from the NAEP state assessments (see Appendix E). In addition to the national NEAP, which is based on a nationally representative sample of students, the state assessments are based on representative sample of public school students selected from participating states. The first section presents the results of NAEP scale score analysis and the second section presents the results of the proficiency rate analysis for individual states.

STATE NAEP READING AND MATH SCALE SCORE TRENDS

Trends in the Average Achievement: The NAEP state assessment has provided information on state-by-state reading and math achievement for grade 4 and grade 8 since 1990. Using data from the NAEP state assessment, a baseline level of performance can be determined for each state, and it can be used to compare states to each other. There is considerable variability among states in baseline scores. Table 7.1 and Table 7.2 classify states based on the results of HLM trend analyses of NAEP 4th grade and 8th grade state average scores in reading and math respectively. As with the national trend, the growth trajectory was divided into pre-NCLB and post-NCLB time periods. In order to test for the statistical significance of the trends, HLM growth modeling analyses of state NAEP reading and math scale

The Testing Gap, pages 109–94

TABLE 7.1
Classification of States in Pre-NCLB and Post-NCLB Trends of NAEP Grade 4 and Grade 8 Reading Average Achievement

| | | Post-NCLB Change | | |
		Increment	Same	Decrement
	Up		CO(4), DE(4), FL(4), MD(4), MO(8), NY(4)	DE(8)
	Flat		AL, AK, AZ, AR, CA, CO (8), CT, FL(8), GA, HI, ID, IL, IN, IA, KS, KY, LA, ME, MD(8), MA, MI, MN, MS, MO(4), MT, NE, NV, NH, NJ, NM, NY(8), NC, ND, OH, OK, OR, PA, RI, SC, SD, TN, TX, UT, VT, VA, WA, WV, WI, WY	
Pre-NCLB Growth	Down			

Note. Numbers in parenthesis refer to grades in which different growth patterns are observed. When the same growth patterns apply to both grades 4 and 8 in each state, no numbers are shown after state code. "Up" means improvement of the average, whereas "Down" means decline of the average.

scores were conducted. Pre-NCLB growth dimension (rows in the Tables 7.1 and 7.2) tells which states changed in which directions before NCLB: up (significantly upward trend), down (significantly downward trend); flat (no significant trend). Post-NCLB change dimension (columns in the Tables 7.1 and 7.2) tells whether and how their pre-NCLB growth pattern changed after NCLB: increment (significant post-NCLB gain); decrement (significant post-NCLB loss); same (no significant change).[1]

In reading, most states did not make progress in improving average scores at both grades levels either before or after NCLB. In math, many states made significant gains at both grades before NCLB, and they continued the same rate of progress (grade 8) or accelerated their progress (grade 4) after NCLB.

Trends in the Achievement Gap: Further, there are also variations among states in racial achievement gap trends. Despite substantial variations in the initial status of the gap at the baseline, the White–Black gap tends to

TABLE 7.2
Classification of States in Pre-NCLB and Post-NCLB Trends of NAEP Grade 4 and Grade 8 Math Average Achievement

| | | Post-NCLB Change | | |
		Increment	Same	Decrement
	Up	AL(4), AZ(4), AR(4), CA(4), CO(4), CT(4), DE(4), FL(4), GA(4), HI(4), ID(4), IN(4), KS(4), KY(4), LA(4), MD(4), MA(4), MI(4), MN(4), MS(4), MO(4), NH(4), NJ(4), NY(4), NC(4), OH(4), OK(4), OR(4), PA(4), RI(4), SC(4), TN(4), TX(4), UT(4), VT(4), VA(4), WA(4), WV(4), WY(4)	AL(8), AZ(8), AR(8), CA(8), CO(8), CT(8), DE(8), FL(8), GA(8), HI(8), ID(8), IL(8), IN(8), KY(8), LA(8), MD(8), MA(8), MI(8), MN(8), MS(8), NH(8), NJ(8), NY(8), NC(8), OH(8), OR(8), PA(8), RI(8), SC(8), TX(8), VA(8), WV(8), WI(8), WY(8)	
Pre-NCLB Growth	Flat	AK(4), IL(4), IA(4), ME(4), MT(4), NE(4), NV(4), NM(4), ND(4), SD(4), WI(4)	AK(8), IA(8), KS(8), ME(8), MO(8), MT(8), NE(8), NV(8), NM(8), ND(8), OK(8), SD(8), TN(8), UT(8), VT(8), WA(8)	
	Down			

Note. Numbers in parenthesis refer to grades in which different growth patterns are observed. When the same growth patterns apply to both grades 4 and 8 in each state, no numbers are shown after state code. "Up" means improvement of the average, whereas "Down" means decline of the average.

remain flat throughout the period for most states. For example, the states' baseline status of grade 4 math White–Black gap as of 1992 varies from 15 points in West Virginia to 42 points in Michigan. However, states do not vary much in their growth rate, as most states made little or no progress in narrowing the gap. Similar patterns continued after NCLB.

Table 7.3 and Table 7.4 classify states based on the results of HLM trend analyses of NAEP 4th grade and 8th grade state average White–Black gaps in reading and math respectively. In grade 8 reading and math, none of

TABLE 7.3

Classification of States in Pre-NCLB and Post-NCLB Trends of NAEP Grade 4 and Grade 8 Reading White–Black Gap

		Post-NCLB Change		
		Increment	Same	Decrement
	Up			
	Flat		AL, AK, AZ, AR, CA, CO, CT, DE, FL, GA, HI, IL, IN, IA, KS, KY, LA, MD, MA, MI, MN, MS, MO, NE, NV, NJ, NM, NY, NC, OH, OK, OR, PA, RI, SC, TN, TX, VA, WA, WV, WI	
Pre-NCLB Growth				
	Down			

Note. Numbers in parenthesis refer to grades in which different growth patterns are observed. When the same growth patterns apply to both grades 4 and 8 in each state, no numbers are shown after state code. "Up" signifies widening of the gap, whereas "Down" signifies narrowing of the gap.

the states changed the White–Black gaps in either the pre-NCLB or post-NCLB period. While there were some variations among states in the amount of changes, they were not significant. States also did not make significant changes in the gap between Poor and Nonpoor students throughout the period. Consequently, racial and socioeconomic achievement gaps did not significantly change after NCLB in most states.

Do the results of this state achievement trend analysis give the same or different information from the national achievement trend analysis as reported in Chapter 6? By and large, the results of combining state-level data also imply divergent trends between reading and math. In reading, only a handful of states made significant gains before NCLB, and none accelerated its growth after NCLB. In math, many states made significant gains on average (except for some racial and socioeconomic groups) throughout the pre-NCLB period at both grade 4 and grade 8. However, post-NCLB progress towards improving math achievement was mixed. Fourth graders' math achievement accelerated since NCLB, while eighth graders' math achievement stayed the same course of growth. The results of this state-level analysis, showing a significant, post-NCLB change in the state average grade 4 math achievement, contrasts with the corresponding national-level aggregate pattern of insignificant post-NCLB change. It

TABLE 7.4
Classification of States in Pre-NCLB and Post-NCLB Trends of NAEP Grade 4 and Grade 8 Math White–Black Gap

		Post-NCLB Change		
		Increment	Same	Decrement
	Up			
	Flat		AL, AK, AZ, AR, CA,	
			CO, CT, DE, FL, GA,	
			HI (4), IL, IN, IA, KS,	
Pre-NCLB			KY, LA, MD, MA, MI,	
Growth			MN(8) MS, MO, NE,	
			NV, NJ, NM, NY, NC,	
			OH, OK, OR, PA, RI,	
			SC, TN, TX, VA, WA,	
			WV, WI	
	Down		MN(4)	

Note. Numbers in parenthesis refer to grades in which different growth patterns are observed. When the same growth patterns apply to both grades 4 and 8 in each state, no numbers are shown after state code. "Up" signifies widening of the gap, whereas "Down" signifies narrowing of the gap.

needs to be noted that significant post-NCLB improvement of grade 4 math achievement in many states occurred mostly between 2000 and 2003 but not between 2003 and 2005; the temporary increase was followed by a return to the pre-reform growth rate. Finally, the results of national and state analyses converge with regard to equity, in that the achievement gaps among racial and socioeconomic groups in both reading and math remained largely unchanged throughout the entire period.

STATE NAEP READING AND MATH PROFICIENCY TRENDS

Trends in the Average Proficiency: Similar patterns are found from the results of HLM analyses that investigate the reading and math trends in proficiency rates using all states' NAEP assessment data throughout the 1990–2005 period and includes both pre-NCLB and post-NCLB time blocks. In both reading and math, there were significant gains made by all racial and socioeconomic groups throughout the period at grade 4 and 8. However, progress was mixed after NCLB. The trend in fourth graders' math achievement has accelerated since NCLB. On the other hand, there were also some significant setbacks after NCLB, including the deceleration of 8th grade reading.

Trends in the Proficiency Gap: The gaps in reading and math proficiency rates among racial and socioeconomic groups remained largely unchanged throughout the period. Exceptions to this pattern were the White–Black gap in 4th grade math and the Nonpoor-Poor gap in 4th and 8th grade reading, both of which narrowed significantly throughout the period. The Nonpoor-Poor gap in grades 4 and 8 reading grew since NCLB while it went down in grade 4 math. All other gaps remained the same and the earlier gap pattern perpetuated since NCLB.

EFFECTS OF STATE ACCOUNTABILITY POLICIES ON THE NAEP READING AND MATH ACHIEVEMENT TRENDS

This study tests the hypothesis that the first generation accountability states that had high-stakes testing and a strong accountability system in the 1990s would have had greater academic improvement before NCLB, whereas the second generation accountability states that lacked such a system in the 1990s would make greater progress after NCLB. To test the hypothesis, this study uses the measure of state accountability constructed by Lee and Wong (2004) (see Appendix A). Based on this accountability policy score, 50 states were also classified into three groups: strong accountability systems (13 states in the top quartile), those with moderate accountability systems (25 states in the middle half), and states with weak accountability systems (12 states in the bottom quartile).[2] Although most weak accountability states also had state assessments, and some even had report cards for schools, none of them provided direct incentives to schools in the form of performance ratings, rewards, assistance, and/or sanctions. This weak accountability group represents the second generation accountability states. In contrast, most strong accountability states turned out to have these key elements of accountability policy in place, and this group represents the first generation accountability states.

If we were to find significantly positive effect of this state accountability variable on pre-NCLB growth, but at the same time significantly negative effect on post-NCLB change, it would support the above hypothesis. Tables F.1 and F.2 in Appendix F summarize the results of HLM analysis on the relationship of state accountability with pre- and post-NCLB reading and math achievement trends at grade 4 and grade 8 respectively.

The Effects of State Accountability on the Average Achievement: Some individual states made relatively larger academic progress than other states, but this progress does not appear to be systematically related to the kinds of state reform variables that might support the hypothesis of long-term test-driven external accountability policy. When pre-NCLB and post-NCLB achievement trends appear to favor test-driven accountability, this phenomenon seems to partly reflect an artifact of regression to the mean; the first generation states were performing low at the baseline and made relatively larger math achievement gains prior to NCLB than the second generation states. Further, the findings imply that NCLB did not work yet as intended to transfer the alleged effects of a test-driven external accountability system to all states.

With consistently insignificant effects in reading, it appears that state accountability policy contributes very little to the interstate variation in the NAEP reading trend, whether it concerns pre-NCLB growth or post-NCLB change. An exception is found in the grade 4 reading trend for Whites only. In contrast, it appears that the state accountability variable contributes partly to the pre-NCLB growth in math but not to the post-NCLB change. In other words, the earlier accountability policy effect on math achievement among the first generation states, if any, fails to have transferred to the second generation states as a result of NCLB as shown by insignificant policy effects on post-NCLB change.

Figure 7.1 shows that the state average NAEP grade 4 math achievement gain prior to NCLB was relatively larger in strong accountability states than in weak accountability states. For example, the HLM estimate of pre-NCLB annual growth rate for Whites was 1.05 in the strong accountability states and .87 in the weak accountability states. This difference in annual gain translates into cumulative gains of 10.5 and 8.7 for each group over the past 10 years prior to NCLB (1992–2001). Although the difference of 1.8

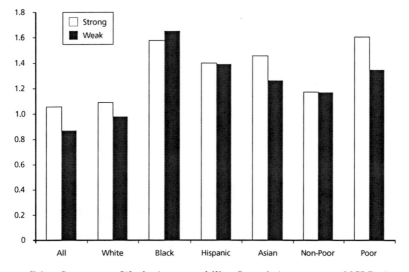

Figure 7.1.   Strong vs. Weak Accountability States' Average pre-NCLB Annual Growth Rates in NAEP Grade 4 Math Achievement by Subgroup.

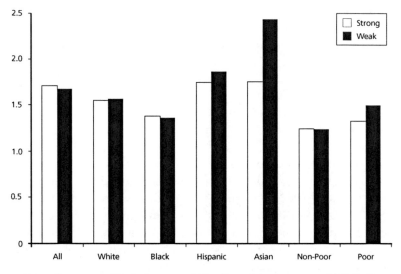

Figure 7.2.   Strong vs. Weak Accountability States' Average post-NCLB Change to Annual Growth Rates in NAEP Grade 4 Math Achievement by Subgroup.

was statistically significant, it may not be of practical import. After adjustment for initial status differences between strong and weak accountability states, significantly positive state accountability policy effect observed prior to NCLB is limited to only Whites in grade 4 math and only Whites and Hispanics in grade 8 math (see Tables F.1 and F.2).

On the other hand, there were no clear indications from the analysis of post-NCLB change patterns (2002–05) that the math achievement of 4th grade students improved more in the second generation states than in the first generation states. Figure 7.2 compares post-NCLB change in the states' average grade 4 math annual growth rates between strong and weak accountability states. For example, the HLM estimate of post-NCLB change in grade 4 math growth rate for Whites was 1.55 in the strong accountability states and 1.56 in the weak accountability states. This difference is not significant, and thus it does not give support for the claim that the states without test-driven external accountability policy before NCLB should benefit more from NCLB than the states with preexisting accountability. While some significant policy effects were observed among Hispanic and Poor students, the relationships turned out to be very tenuous once we take into account for differences in initial status and pre-NCLB growth rate (see Table F.1 and Table F.2).

The Effects of State Accountability on the Achievement Gap: Further, HLM analyses were also conducted to test the effects of accountability policies on racial and socioeconomic achievement gaps. The results of HLM analyses suggest that although the strong accountability states such as Texas with initially larger achievement gaps appear to have narrowed some of the gaps more than their weak accountability counterparts before NCLB, there is no significant difference between the two groups of states once their initial difference was considered. Further, there is no indication that the gaps narrowed more or less in one group of states than the other after NCLB.

By and large, state accountability was not significantly related to pre-NCLB growth and post-NCLB changes in the racial and socioeconomic gaps. In both reading and math, few states changed the gaps significantly over the entire period, and there were no systematic differences between strong accountability states and weak accountability states in terms of changes in achievement gaps for Blacks and Hispanics as well as for Poor students. For example, Texas, one of strong accountability states, appears to have made some progress between 1990/92 and 2005 in narrowing the White–Black gap (1 point increase in grade 4 reading; 5 point decrease in grade 4 math; 7 point decrease in grade 8 math) and the White-Hispanic gap (1 point decrease in grade 4 reading; 3 point decrease in grade 4 math; 4 point decrease in grade 8 math). Progress is also seen in the state's narrowing the Nonpoor-Poor gap between 1996/98 and 2005 (5 point decrease in grade 4 reading and math, 2 point decrease in grade 8 reading; 5 point decrease in grade 8 math). Considering initially large gaps at the baseline (e.g., 38 points for White–Black gap and 28 points for White-Hispanic gap in 1990 grade 8 math), however, these reductions only account for 4–20 percent of the initial gaps.

CONCLUSION

In the past, few states have been able to narrow racial and socioeconomic achievement gaps while improving overall achievement levels at the same time. If NCLB can facilitate the systemic efforts of state education systems to close pernicious achievement gaps, this would be noteworthy. By and large, the results of state-level NAEP trend analyses imply that NCLB's attempt to scale up the alleged success of the first generation accountability states (e.g., Florida, North Carolina, Texas) have so far not been effective. NCLB neither enhanced the first generation states' earlier academic improvement nor transferred the effects of their test-driven accountability policy to the second generation accountability states. The first generation accountability states made relatively greater academic progress before NCLB in math but not in reading. Moreover, the relatively larger math gains among the first generation states were not sustained after NCLB. More importantly, states that adopted test-driven external accountability either before or after NCLB did not reduce racial and socioeconomic inequalities in reading and math achievement. It is evident that test-driven external accountability, whether it was a state or federal initiative, has not advanced equity on a large scale, as the disparity in achievement among different racial and socioeconomic groups of students persists before and after NCLB. Nevertheless, I acknowledge that only four years of post-NCLB data are available and thus it may be premature to come to final conclusion. Reform initiatives, especially large-scale federal ones, may take longer to work. The results remain suggestive and despite no clear signs of changes, the future trends need to be carefully followed.

NOTES

1. For racial minority groups, the number of states is less than 50 since the NAEP test results for Asians, Blacks and/or Hispanics in certain states are not available due to insufficient sample size of the groups for reliable estimation. For each minority group, states that are not included in the Tables are as follows:

    (1) Asian
    Alabama, Arizona (except grade 4 reading and math), Arkansas, Idaho, Indiana, Iowa (except grade 4 reading), Kentucky, Louisiana, Maine, Michigan (except grade 4 math), Mississippi, Missouri, Montana, Nebraska, New Hampshire, New Mexico, North Dakota, Ohio, Oklahoma (except grade 4 math), Pennsylvania (except grade 4 reading, grade 8 reading and math), South Carolina, South Dakota, Tennessee, Vermont, West Virginia, and Wyoming.

    (2) Black
    Hawaii (except grade 4 reading and math, grade 8 reading), Idaho, Maine, Montana, New Hampshire, North Dakota, South Dakota, Utah, Vermont, and Wyoming

    (3) Hispanic
    Alabama, Kentucky, Louisiana, Maine, Mississippi, Missouri (except grade 4 reading and math, grade 8 reading), Montana (except grade 4 reading and math), New Hampshire (except grade 4 reading and math), North Dakota, South Carolina (except grade 4 reading and math, grade 8 math), South Dakota (except grade 4 math), Tennessee (except grade 4 reading and math), Vermont, and West Virginia.

2. States with strong accountability systems include Alabama, Florida, Illinois, Indiana, Kentucky, Louisiana, Maryland, New Jersey, New Mexico, New York, North Carolina, and Texas. In contrast, states with weak accountability systems include Alaska, Arkansas, Colorado, Delaware, Idaho, Iowa, Maine, Massachusetts, Montana, Nebraska, New Hampshire, North Dakota, and Wyoming. Strong accountability states are more likely to be the first-generation accountability states, whereas weak accountability are more likely to be the second-generation accountability states which did not have statewide high-stakes testing and accountability systems until NCLB.

CHAPTER 8

DISCREPANCIES BETWEEN NAEP AND STATE ASSESSMENT RESULTS

NCLB requires each state to develop a test-based accountability system to monitor the performance of schools and districts. Each state administers its own assessments and establishes performance targets that students must meet.[1] Although NCLB establishes state assessments as the basis for NCLB accountability, NAEP can play a confirmatory role as an independent assessment to validate the state test results. Previous studies revealed discrepancies between NAEP and state assessment results in terms of the level of student achievement, as well as in the size of statewide achievement gains (Fuller et al., 2006; Klein et al., 2000; Koretz & Barron, 1998; Lee, in press-b; Linn et al., 2002). For example, the RAND study of Texas (Klein et al., 2000) reported that fourth grade reading scores improved about three times faster on Texas Assessment of Academic Skills (TAAS) than on NAEP between 1994 and 1998: the 4-year gains in standard deviation units on TAAS vs. NAEP were 0.31 vs. 0.13 for Whites, 0.49 vs. 0.14 for Blacks, and 0.39 vs. 0.14 for Hispanics. This study challenged the earlier report of Texas miracle based on TAAS results and achieved notoriety after being released two weeks prior to the 2000 presidential election (Fuller et al., 2006). While some raised concerns about the content of NAEP test as a gold standard to judge the validity of state test (see Loveless, 2006), NAEP remains the most useful tool with common frame of reference based on national standards for cross-checking different states' test results.

Building upon the previous studies, this chapter updates results by expanding the analysis to post-NCLB test results across 50 states. Using two measures of states' academic performance (states' own assessments and the NAEP state assessments), the first section compares the percentage of students meeting or exceeding the proficiency standard in reading and math set by each state with the percentage of students meeting or exceeding the NAEP proficiency standard. Separate results are reported for racial and socioeconomic subgroups. Secondly, the role of state accountability policy in fostering improvements in student achievement is explored by examining variations among states in the patterns of discrepancies between NAEP and state assessment in the average proficiency and the achievement gap. Finally, further comparison is made between NAEP and state assessment with regard to post-NCLB academic progress as measured by the state average proficiency gains.

NAEP VERSUS STATE ASSESSMENT RESULTS ON THE AVERAGE PROFICIENCY AND THE GAP

The percentages of students meeting or exceeding the proficiency standard in both reading and math were, on average, twice as large, and in some cases, even larger, on state assessments than on the NAEP. This implies that for most states, NAEP performance standards are more challenging than are the states' own (see Table G.1 in Appendix G for a measure of the discrepancies between NAEP and state assessments in reading and math proficiency for each state). Figures 8.1 and 8.2 illustrate the discrepancies between NAEP scores and performance on state assessments in grade 4 reading and math respectively. There were discrepancies between the NEAP and state assessments for every racial group; the discrepancy tends to be especially large for Blacks (about 4 times larger) and Hispanics (about 3 times larger) in comparison with Whites and Asians (about 2 times larger). The discrepancies also existed for economic subgroups: Poor (about 3 times) and Nonpoor (about 2 times). This suggests that the discrepancies between NAEP and state assessment may have been larger for disadvantaged and minority groups than for advantaged and White groups. These uneven patterns of the discrepancies may result because the disadvantaged and minority groups include more low-achieving students who could have passed state standard, but not the more rigorous NAEP standard.

Table 8.1 summarizes the discrepancies between NAEP and state assessments across states for all students and each subgroup by subject and grade. The discrepancy between the two assessments is a ratio of the state assessment-based estimate of proficiency rate to the NAEP-based estimate

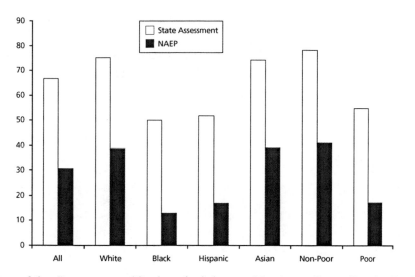

Figure 8.1.   Percentages of Students by Subgroup Meeting or Exceeding the Proficiency Standard in Grade 4 Reading on State Assessment vs. NAEP.

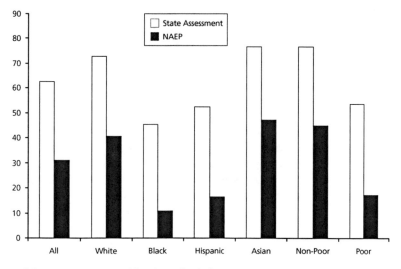

Figure 8.2.   Percentages of Students by Subgroup Meeting or Exceeding the Proficiency Standard in Grade 4 Math on State Assessment vs. NAEP.

of proficiency rate. The more this ratio departs from the value of one, the greater the discrepancies between the two assessments. When the ratio exceeds 1, it suggests that state standards are lower than the NEAP standards, whereas a ratio below 1 suggests that state standards are relatively higher than the NAEP standards.[2] In all cases, the ratio is larger than 1,

TABLE 8.1
Discrepancies between NAEP and State Assessment Results in Grade 4 and Grade 8 Reading and Math (N = 43 states)

	Ratio of state-assessment proficiency rate to NAEP proficiency rate			
	Grade 4		Grade 8	
	Reading	Math	Reading	Math
All	2.25	2.10	2.02	1.95
White	1.98	1.85	1.86	1.80
Black	4.12	4.66	3.61	4.47
Hispanic	3.29	3.64	3.08	3.30
Asian	2.05	1.75	1.83	1.72
Nonpoor	1.93	1.73	1.87	1.80
Poor	3.33	3.37	2.95	3.31
White–Black gap	.55	.45	.60	.53
White–Hispanic gap	.65	.57	.69	.62
Poverty gap	.63	.57	.73	.63

Note. For all and subgroups, the average ratio of state assessment-based proficiency rate to NAEP-based proficiency rate was calculated across all available states and years. For the racial gap, an odds ratio was calculated by dividing the ratio of White proficiency rate to Black or Hispanic proficiency rate based on state assessment by its corresponding ratio based on NAEP. Likewise, an odds ratio was calculated for the poverty gap by dividing the ratio of Nonpoor proficiency rate to Poor proficiency rate based on state assessment by its corresponding ratio based on NAEP.

suggesting that state standards are lower than NAEP standards. The discrepancies between NAEP and state assessment results are the largest for Black, Hispanic and Poor students and the smallest for White and Nonpoor students. These findings are consistent across grades and in both reading and math. This suggests that Blacks, Hispanic and Poor students are less likely to meet the proficiency standard than White and Nonpoor students, and the proficiency gap tends to be larger with the NAEP standard than with the state standard.

Compared to the NAEP, state assessments tend to underestimate the racial and socioeconomic achievement gap. This finding is related to uneven patterns of NAEP vs. state assessment discrepancies in proficiency rates for different racial and socioeconomic groups. As shown in the bottom of Table 8.1, the estimate of the achievement gap between Black and White students obtained from state assessments is half the Black–White achievement gap estimated by NAEP. For example, the White–Black gap in grade 4 math based on the state assessment was 1.8; the percentage of students meeting or exceeding the proficiency standard was 1.8 times greater for Whites than for Blacks. In contrast, the corresponding White–Black gap based on NAEP was 4.3; the percentage of students scoring at or above Proficient was 4.3 times greater for Whites than for Blacks. Consequently, the estimate of White–Black proficiency gap based on state assessment was only half of the gap estimate based on NAEP (.45 for grade 4 math White–Black gap in Table 8.1). Likewise, the estimate of the achievement gap between Hispanic and White students obtained from state assessments is two-thirds of the estimate of the Hispanic–White achievement gap estimated by NAEP. The same pattern of discrepancy is found for the Nonpoor-Poor achievement gap.

EFFECTS OF STATE ACCOUNTABILITY ON THE DIVERGENCE OF NAEP AND STATE ASSESSMENT RESULTS

While the aforementioned findings reflect typical nationwide patterns, there are interstate variations in the discrepancies between NAEP proficiency standards and state proficiency standards. One factor that may explain these observed variations among states is the degree to which consequences (rewards or sanctions) are attached to state test results for schools and students. This study hypothesizes that the states that have high-stakes testing and a strong accountability system would exert greater pressure for schools and students to improve their achievement on the state test than states without high-stakes accountability systems. High stakes accountability results in the possible inflation of the number of students reaching the proficiency level and thus a deflation of the achievement gap. The state education agency itself is also likely to water down its own performance standards in anticipation of massive failure. To test the hypothesis, this study uses the measure of state accountability constructed by Lee and Wong (2004) (see Appendix A for description of the variable).

Correlation analysis supports the hypothesis that proficiency levels in states with high-stakes testing and accountability systems are inflated. We find a positive relationship between the level of state accountability and the size of NAEP-state assessment discrepancies. The discrepancies between state proficiency levels and NEAP proficiency levels are particularly large in math. The results are presented in Figure 8.3 and in Table G.2 in Appendix G, which summarizes the results of correlation analysis by grade and subject.

The results indicate that the higher the stakes attached to state assessments, the lower the states' own performance standards relative to NAEP standards. Figure 8.1 illustrates this relationship among 43 states by displaying the level of state accountability (horizontal axis) and the size of dis-

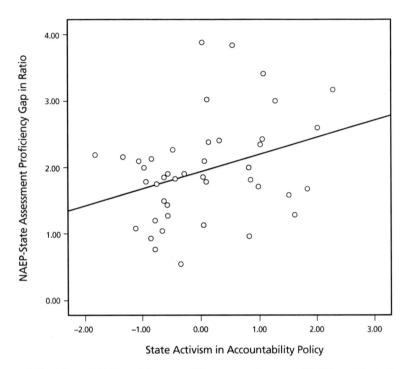

Figure 8.3.   Plot of 43 States' Average Discrepancy between NAEP and State Assessment in the 8th Grade Math Proficiency (vertical axis) vs. Test-driven External Accountability Policy (horizontal axis).

crepancy between NAEP and state assessments in grade 8 math proficiency rate (vertical axis): the correlation between two variables is significantly positive ($r = .36$). For example, the stakes for failing to meet the state's performance targets are higher in Kentucky than in Maine. In 2003, 31% of students were proficient in grade 8 math on Kentucky's state test versus 24% that were proficient on the NAEP. As a result, the discrepancy between the NAEP and state assessment is 1.3 (the ratio of 31 to 24) in Kentucky. This suggests that the performance standards for the Kentucky Core Content Test (KCCT) have been set at relatively lower levels than the standards for NAEP. In contrast, the performance standards for the Maine Education Assessment (MEA) have been set at relatively higher levels than the standards for NAEP. In 2003, 18% of students met or exceeded the standard in grade 8 math on the Maine state test, whereas 29% of students scored proficient on the NAEP. This results in the discrepancy of 0.6 (ratio of 18 to 29 in Maine).

Further, there are indications that states with high-stakes accountability systems show relatively smaller racial achievement gaps on their own state tests than on NAEP. The correlation analysis supports the hypothesis that high stakes testing tends to deflate achievement gaps. The stronger test-driven external accountability, the smaller the discrepancies between NAEP and state assessment for achievement gaps, particularly White–Black gap in math. For example, the correlation between the level of state accountability and the size of discrepancy between NAEP and state assessment in grade 8 math White–Black gap was significantly negative ($r = -.36$).

NAEP VERSUS STATE ASSESSMENT RESULTS ON POST-NCLB PROFICIENCY GAINS

There is also the possibility that there is a discrepancy between the state assessment results and NAEP results in the amount of academic progress students made before NCLB and after NCLB. Unfortunately, currently available state assessment data are limited in their time span (typically available for up to the last 3–5 years) so that it is not possible to trace the pre-NCLB trend in most cases. Therefore, only the post-NCLB trend was compared in this study.

To determine if student progress on state assessments differed from student progress on NAEP, average gains in statewide proficiency rates from 2003 to 2005 was calculated for each state for both NAEP and state assessments. There were 25 states that had 2005 state reading and math assessment results available on their state education department web sites by the end of 2005.[3] Figures 8.4 and 8.5 illustrate the discrepancies in grade 8 proficiency gain estimates in reading and math respectively based on NAEP

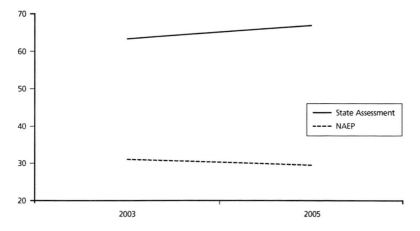

Figure 8.4.   2003–05 Grade 8 Reading Proficiency Trends based on State Assessment vs. NAEP (N = 25 states).

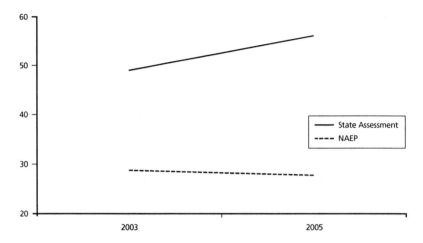

Figure 8.5.   2003–05 Grade 8 Math Proficiency Trend based on State Assessment vs. NAEP (N = 25 states).

and state assessments. It shows that the gain was greater on the state assessments than on NAEP for those 25 states. In both grades 4 and 8 reading and in grade 8 math, there was no progress or a slight decline on NAEP, whereas there was some positive gain on the state assessments. In grade 4 math, both assessments showed progress, but the size of gain was smaller on NAEP. Table G.3 in Appendix G summarizes the results by each subject and grade.

Although there can be other reasons for these discrepancies between NAEP and state assessments in the size of estimated achievement gain scores, the gaps may be attributable partly to the fact that state assessment results are the basis of school accountability decisions under NCLB. High-stakes testing situations can lead to the possible inflation of achievement gains since schools may focus on teaching to the test as opposed to adopting changes that lead to genuine progress in learning. In the long term, NAEP and state assessment results may converge as a result of the increasing role of NAEP as a confirmatory tool and thus we may see greater alignment of state assessment results with NAEP under NCLB (Lee, in press).

If we assume that the states stay on the above NAEP performance trajectories and thus continue to make the same amount of gains as they did during the 2003–05 period, it is projected that by 2014 only 32 percent of 4th graders and 23 percent of 8th graders would meet the reading proficiency target and about 56 percent of 4th graders and 24 percent of 8th graders would meet the math proficiency target. In contrast, projections based on state assessment trends would project that 95 percent of 4th graders and 82 percent of 8th graders would meet the reading proficiency target and 94 percent of 4th graders and 88 percent of 8th graders would meet the math proficiency target. Although the projections based on both NAEP and state assessments fall short of the 100 percent proficiency target, the feasibility of reaching the proposed goal diverges greatly between NAEP and state assessment.

CONCLUSION

One approach to closing the achievement gap may focus on each racial or socioeconomic subgroup's performance relative to a desired proficiency standard. In this view, the progress of Black, Hispanic, or Poor student subgroups towards the standard is evaluated on its own merits, and passing a designated threshold will be treated as narrowing the gap regardless of how the subgroup does in comparison to the White or Nonpoor subgroups. This approach is implied in NCLB, as the goal is to have every student meet a desired performance standard. If we adopt such a criterion-referenced view of closing the gap, we may observe a subgroup continuing to make progress toward the proficiency goal. However, meeting a pre-set threshold conveys no information about the achievement gap, and only provides information on whether or not a particular goal is reached. If the proficiency level is set so that the vast majority of Whites are over it at the beginning of the period studied, any improvement of minority students' proficiency rate may misleadingly signify progress toward closing the gap and obscure the relative gap between racial groups. This is of particular concern since NCLB establishes state assessments as the basis for school accountability and state standards vary widely in relationship to NAEP standards.

Despite the increasing importance of NAEP as the source of information for national and state report cards, the current practice of using states' own student assessments for school accountability purposes requires us to investigate the adequacy and utility of both assessments. In comparison with NAEP, state assessments tend to inflate the overall proficiency level and at the same time deflate the achievement gap among racial groups. This poses a threat to the validity of inferences based solely on states' own standards and assessment results. The results imply that the first generation accountability states with high-stakes testing policies in place prior to NCLB have adopted relatively lower performance standards, leading to overestimation of their proficiency rates and underestimation of the achievement gap. The findings also suggest that policy-makers become more aware of potential biases resulting from relying exclusively on states' own test measure for accountability.

NOTES

1. While many states adopted achievement levels that are very similar to NAEP levels, the labels of achievement levels vary among states.

2. For comparison of the assessment results related to achievement levels, this study only examines the level of achievement defined by the states as meeting desired performance standards under NCLB. On NAEP, student achievement at or above "Proficient" is treated as meeting or exceeding the national standard. For the proficiency gap among racial and socioeconomic groups, a ratio greater than 1 implies state overestimation of the gap, relative NAEP, while a ratio less than 1 implies underestimation of the gap.

3. This number includes states that gave state assessments to the same grade as NAEP (grade 4 and grade 8) or adjacent grades: Alaska, Arizona, California, Colorado, Delaware, Georgia, Hawaii, Idaho, Indiana, Kansas, Louisiana, Maine, Maryland, Massachusetts, Michigan, Mississippi, Missouri, Nevada, New Jersey, North Carolina, Ohio, Pennsylvania, South Dakota, Virginia, and Washington.

PART III

TRANSFORMING THE FUTURE OF EDUCATIONAL ACCOUNTABILITY SYSTEM

CHAPTER 9

CONCLUSION

REVISITING TEST-DRIVEN EXTERNAL ACCOUNTABILITY UNDER NCLB

School is a place where the future grows. Education should help improve and transform the future lives of all children by providing them with excellent and equitable learning opportunities. Therefore, it is imperative that schools must be held accountable for providing excellent and equitable education for all. Educational policymakers, businessmen, news media, and the public often attempt to judge the quality of public schools by test scores or other readily available evidence. When they are led to believe that test scores decline over time or poorly compare with other countries, they press for public school reform with demand for improved test results of student achievement. Although a test-driven school accountability system has the potential to help schools achieve desired educational goals, the ways in which it is currently designed, implemented and evaluated may threaten the future.

In the midst of the international brain race, many nation-states have played a leading role in education reform for developing human capital that gives them a competitive edge over other countries in a global economy. The United States is one of the nations that was highly active in public school reform over the past two decades by raising curriculum and performance standards to improve academic excellence. However, setting and pursuing unrealistically high goals without sufficient support could bring about an endless cycle of educational crisis and futile school reform.[1] Being the top-ranking nation in math and science achievement as envi-

The Testing Gap, pages 131–120
Copyright © 2007 by Information Age Publishing
All rights of reproduction in any form reserved.

sioned by Goals 2000 is an example of an unrealistic policy goal that was set to fail by design.

Past behavior is often the best predictor of future behavior. NCLB mandates 100 percent proficiency for all students including racial minorities and economically disadvantaged groups. Is this policy mission impossible? Will NCLB become just another example of policy failure due to such an unrealistically lofty goal? Critics of NCLB claim that from the beginning the idea of performance-driven accountability was an explicitly political idea and it was weak on practical details. Indeed, the findings of this book challenge the feasibility of NCLB goals and rebut claims that test-driven external accountability works to help close the achievement gap. External, test-driven accountability relies on state-imposed high-stakes testing with rewards and/or sanctions to improve test results as indicators of teacher and school performance. Although this type of accountability has been popular in the United States during the last decade and may become a national prototype of accountability as a result of the NCLB, it is very limited in its nature and design.

Under NCLB, states set the standards, choose a test to measure student performance against the standards, and hold schools accountable for the results. Under these circumstances, high-stakes testing works not only as an intervention but also as an instrument to measure the outcome of the intervention. On one hand, high-stakes testing generates enormous pressure for educators to improve test scores by means of narrowing the curriculum and teaching to the test. On the other hand, any inflated test scores that can result from intensive drilling and coaching under this pressure generates an illusion of real progress and gives the false impression that the intervention is working. Then this situation will prompt more investment into high-stakes testing and further prescribed curriculum. However, the same amount of achievement gains do not appear when students take an independent low-stakes test such as NAEP. In combination with other threats, this "testing gap" raises serious questions about the validity of state testing programs for school accountability.

Even small gains for minority students on state assessments may create the illusion of progress under NCLB. However, we need to look back at the history of progress in narrowing the racial achievement gap over the past 3 decades. The gaps narrowed substantially in the 1970s and 1980s but then stopped narrowing or widened in the 1990s. Any progress we may see after NCLB may loom large in light of this recent stagnation. However, this post-NCLB gain is much smaller than the earlier gains that the nation made earlier. In the past, education and social policies worked to narrow the achievement gap by guaranteeing a minimally adequate level of achievement for minorities through compensatory education, minimum competency testing, school desegregation, equalization of school funding, the War on Poverty, and affirmative action. As the goal has shifted to closing the gap at more advanced knowledge and at a higher-order skills level, improvement of social and educational conditions for minority students did not catch up with the pace.

It is possible that NCLB will produce better results on state assessment than on NAEP over the long run. However, even with state assessment, the current trend predicts that the results will be far short of the target. Some may argue that accumulation of small progress over time will produce the most positive results. I am very skeptical about the claim that it simply takes more time to get the results. In grade 4 math, there was a temporary gain after NCLB but it returned back to the pre-reform growth rate. This indicates that any short-term impact with a large influx of new fund and momentum is not sustainable. One may argue for an even stronger federal dosage of test-driven accountability but it could lead to a situation like "drill and kill": continuous testing practice due to rewards/sanctions will lead to killing motivation for genuine learning and academic progress. The challenge for a new American school accountability system is to provide standards-based education without overstandardization.

The findings of this study also imply that the federal government faces a serious challenge when scaling up test-driven accountability as a policy intervention. There was some limited success of first generation states on NAEP math. But it may have worked under the conditions that are favorable to high-stakes testing in the first-generation states, such as strong top-down leadership, a highly centralized school system, a tradition of minimum competency testing, educational culture with teacher priorities on academic goals, and poor schooling conditions and student outcomes that drive relatively quicker, cheaper and easier-to-implement external interventions. But when the federal government tried to spread this policy to all states, it appears that the effect did not transfer due to very different conditions and culture in the second-generation states.

There remain substantial variations among states in the definitions and levels of student proficiency and teacher qualification, and in the adequacy and equity of school funding.[2] Given the fact that federal funding for public education still makes up less than 10 percent of total educational spending, it remains an outstanding issue how the nation can narrow the gap among states in their different growth trajectories toward the uniform goal of 100 percent proficiency in reading and math.[3]

We should maintain the requirement that test scores be disaggregated and tracked by race and other background characteristics. However, substantial disparities in educational opportunities among racial and socioeconomic groups within states have not been adequately addressed. If NCLB revises the current course of test-driven accountability with shifts to more realistic goals and greater support for disadvantaged high-minority schools and puts forth a series of systemic reform efforts for continued improvement of educational opportunities on the equity front, it may be that NCLB will produce more positive results.

IMPACT OF ACCOUNTABILITY POLICY ON EQUITY

Clearly there are challenges to advancing academic excellence without losing sight of equity. Does American test-driven external accountability boost achievement for low-income, minority students and narrow their achievement gap? The analysis of NAEP data shows that there was no discernable negative effect of accountability on minority or low-income students' achievement and that accountability did not widen their achievement gaps. This can be good news in light of many concerns raised about potentially negative effects of accountability on equity. However, pointing out this fact is not a compliment to states; rather, it is a challenge, given the fact that existing inequalities of educational opportunities remain significant and the resulting achievement gaps are unacceptably large. While this study focused on the racial and socioeconomic achievement gap trends for equity issues, subsequent studies needs to examine any emerging impact of NCLB on the other groups of students who are newly included in state testing programs for accountability purpose, that is, students with disabilities and immigrant students with limited English proficiency.

During the past decade, federal and state activism in test-driven school accountability policy was not accompanied by significant systemic improvements in schooling environment and resources (e.g., safe/orderly climate, collective support, per-pupil expenditures, class size, and qualified teachers). Although improving the adequacy or equity of educational opportunities and resources was not at all the goal of external accountability policy, it was expected that states would play a stronger role in giving all schools and students adequate and fair support commensurate with the enormous pressure and uneven threats that the policy change involved. While accountability policy did not hurt adequacy or equity in schooling conditions, very limited progress was reported. Furthermore, federal and state activism in accountability policy did not bring significant changes in the distribution of student achievement outcomes.

Although this study found no evidence that accountability policy brings about any significant progress or setback toward equity in student learning results, the policy's long-term effect remains to be examined. The long-term effect of accountability on equity may be different from its short-term effect. In other words, some policies may still be too recent to have taken effect. Student accountability polices may have more immediate impact, such as making academic promotion or graduation dependent on test performance. School accountability policies may take longer. States' reports on school performance may not translate immediately into real sanctions. Rather, there may be sanctions after 3–5 years of failing performance. In other words, state accountability systems vary in the actual and immediate application of "high stakes" measures. There are only two or three years of NAEP or state assessment data available for post NCLB analysis. It may be premature to evaluate the full impact of NCLB as the policy sets 2014 as the deadline for states to meet its performance targets.[4] Nevertheless, we should not hesitate to diagnose and fix parts of the system along the way, lest the entire system breaks down.

This study is also limited in linking federal and state policy (policy adoption at the federal/state level rather than attempts at policy implementation at the district and school levels) with changes in the achievement gap. The evidence from large-scale data analyses with primary focus on interstate comparison of student outcomes needs to be balanced with findings from the case studies of policy implementation processes and outcomes at the district, school, and classroom levels. To fill the chasm between what transpires at the state level and what ultimately takes shape as achievement gaps at the student level, subsequent research needs to take into account key school and classroom factors that can influence such multilevel policy-outcome linkages.

While one should interpret the findings from this study about the impact of NCLB cautiously, the study has implications for the debate about reauthorization. NCLB requires adequate yearly progress of all groups of students toward the state proficiency target. The report demonstrates how, over the past few years since NCLB's inception, state assessment results show improvements in math and reading, but students are not showing similar gains on the NAEP—the only independent national test. If we continue the current policy course, academic proficiency is unlikely to improve significantly, but it is possible that the state assessment will continue to give a false impression of progress, shortchanging our children and encouraging more investment into a failed test-driven accountability reform policy. This problem can be more serious for schools that serve predominantly disadvantaged minority students. NCLB has shortchanged those schools with under-funded mandates and an over reliance on sanctions rather than a focus on capacity-building.

IMPLICATIONS FOR REDESIGNING EDUCATIONAL ACCOUNTABILITY SYSTEM

The findings of this study have implications for the design and implementation of test-driven external accountability policy, the hallmark of NCLB, to improve both academic excellence and equity simultaneously. The cure can be worse than the disease under NCLB. The problem in closing the achievement gap is that the gap comes from many different sources including home as well as school. The gap starts even before students enter schools. Parents are the key partners to improve education. Under NCLB, parents have the choice to transfer when their kid's school is in trouble by poor test results. This makes schools lose better-educated and more supportive parents who are more likely to leave the school. Early childhood intervention like universal pre-K is needed. When students enter school, there are also disparities among schools in teacher quality and instructional resources. Under NCLB, the threat of sanctions for low-performing schools makes highly qualified teachers in those schools move to better schools, worsening the shortage of qualified teachers in inner-city, high-poverty, predominantly minority schools. NCLB tries to fix schools after they fail. But this is like fixing the barn door after a horse is stolen. We should not wait to help schools until they fail repeatedly. If we address the disparities among schools before children start schools, sanctions wouldn't be necessary.

How can standards-based educational accountability policies overcome these interlocking problems to improve academic excellence and insure equity? We need to redefine the concept of educational accountability from a broader, systemic and symmetric perspective. The central question for accountability decision-making may be posed: "Who is held accountable for what, how and why?" Assuming that desirable curriculum and performance standards are in place, I recommend new directions for changes in educational accountability systems for enhanced excellence and equity.[5]

Regarding the choice of "whom" to target for accountability, it should involve all parties of education, with more appropriate balance of responsibilities between students and teachers, between home and school, and between policymakers and implementors. When we examine many environmental factors to determine the causes of the achievement gap among different racial and socioeconomic groups of students, we find that academic achievement is influenced by so many interrelated factors simultaneously and it is almost impossible to disentangle the effect of one factor from another. Despite the expectations of shared responsibility or symmetric accountability for academic improvement, concerns about exclusive focus on educators and ignorance of other responsible parties have been raised. The target of NCLB accountability focuses on schools and there is an asymmetry of responsibility and pressure. Policymakers need to be held accountable for providing adequate support to implement enacted policies. Internal accountability must precede external accountability. Policy support should focus on improving the climate and capacity of schools as professional communities to make academic improvements, particularly the beliefs and practices that teachers in the schools share. In order to effectively change student behaviors and outcomes, accountability policy should involve ways to change students as well as teachers.[6]

In addition, accountability should actively involve external community organizations as well as parents as collaborative change agents.[7] Under NCLB, parents can have rights to request supplemental education for their children when their current schools are failing to meet academic performance target. The district in need of improvement should offer supplemental educational services to low-income students through private organizations including for-profit learning centers and community organizations. An early study of policy implementation, however, pointed out lack of interests on the side of parents and students and lack of accountability on the side of school districts and service providers.[8]

Regarding the choice of instruments ("how") for accountability, both inducement and capacity-building have been used as policy tools less frequently by states than mandates. The problem is that incentives and assistance are not only rarely offered, but are also allocated in a way that benefits only those who are already highly motivated and well-prepared for teaching and learning. This may be an efficient way of allocating resources for economic productivity, but runs the risk of aggravating existing inequity and worsening social welfare. For example, merit pay may turn out to reward and empower teachers who already have enough willingness and ability to meet high standards. Likewise, a voucher plan may end up improving the chance of attending high quality schools for students who already have the motivation and aptitude to meet high standards. In contrast to such market-based approaches to educational improvement, the system I propose above should promote fair and reciprocal ways of allocating instructional resources and producing quality learning. At the same time, this approach is also different from past policies aimed toward promoting equal access to essential services or providing compensatory services in that it rests more on the need for quality instruction and aims at providing the enabling conditions for effective teaching and learning rather than controlling the process of schooling.

NCLB should attempt to ensure that Title I schools have comparable resources by requiring states and districts to equalize the distribution of school funding and highly qualified teachers across schools. At the same time, however, we need to address concerns in relation to these policy efforts. For the equalization of school funding, we should acknowledge that there can be areas of inefficiencies in current school spending and increased funding does not guarantee improved student performance in those inefficient schools. It is necessary to strengthen the connection between school resources and performance so that the adequate level of school funding can be established firmly.[9] For the equalization of highly qualified teachers, we should not only provide more incentives to attract new teachers to schools in need of improvement but also try to minimize unintended effect of current accountability system that makes it more difficult to retain experienced teachers in low-performing schools.[10] Moreover, continuous teacher support through mentoring and professional development is essential. Highly qualified teachers who by definition demonstrate subject matter knowledge through teacher certification exams or other means are not necessarily highly effective teachers who actually help improve student achievement. There remain political obstacles as well as technical challenges in using a valued-added growth model to measure the effects of teachers on student achievement.

Regarding the choice of "what" to measure and improve for accountability, we need to keep balance between school inputs and student outcomes and to revise the current measures of school performance. The relation between educational inputs, processes, and outcomes needs to be viewed as an integrated system of teaching and learning. The studies suggest that the states can make greater academic progress when they combine a performance-guarantee approach with an input-guarantee approach. It appears that NCLB follows this path by combining the two approaches in the sense that it requires not only high performance standards for every student with high-stakes testing but also highly qualified teachers in every classroom with more targeted funding. NCLB also encourages evidence-based practice in teaching by supporting curriculum and instructional models that were proven to be effective. However, NCLB shortchanges many states with under-funded mandates, while there remain substantial interstate variations in their capacity for meeting the goal of 100 percent proficiency target.

To make accountability work effectively, we also need to overcome technical challenges related to the use of testing and measurement. The validity and reliability of current test measures and their uses for accountability purposes needs to be improved. While most states use proficiency rates as measures of school performance under NCLB, they do not capture value-added contributions of schools to improvement of student achievement. We should revamp the current AYP rule for school accountability by shifting the focus of performance measurement from status to progress. This may allow states to adopt a growth model voluntarily within certain parameters. Further, we need to set much more realistic performance goals and timeline. However, this AYP reform should be preceded by efforts to address existing disparities among states in the level and rigor of proficiency standards and their time lag for meeting the 100 percent proficiency target. The new goal and timeline of AYP should take national views on standards and capitalize on student achievement results based on NAEP as well as states' own standards and assessments. The federal government may provide incentives for states to align their standards and tests with national ones, and to reinforce the use of NAEP as a confirmatory tool.[11] It is necessary to guard against potential bias such as the inflation of proficiency levels and gains that may result from state's own high-stakes testing.

One approach that policymakers can consider to make the AYP targets more realistic and fair might be to adopt more than one performance standard (Proficient) and to recognize academic progress below the Proficient level. Major concerns are that the state's emphasis on Proficiency as its "gold standard" overlooks the progress made by lower-performing students who meet or exceed the minimum competency level and has a chilling effect on teachers who have moved a significant number of students above that basic level.

Another approach is to use an effect size measure for setting realistic AYP targets. For example, one might reasonably expect that schools should make progress every year by say 20% of the standard deviation of school-level percent proficient measure; for example, this amounts to about 2.5–3.0 percent in Kentucky and 1.5–2.0 percent in Maine. This amount of progress may be regarded as small by conventional statistical standard, but it is exactly what an average school in many states managed to accomplish in the past. In a similar vein, one can consider setting the safe harbor threshold for a subgroup at certain percentage of the standard deviation (e.g., reduce the percentage of non-proficient low-income students by 10% of the standard deviation).[12] The current uniform schedule of meeting a common performance target for all subgroups may be adjusted until equitable learning conditions and opportunities are guaranteed.

Regarding the choice of "why", we need to revisit the goals of accountability and examine reasons for policy success or failure in achieving the goals. During the past two decades, the focus of educational policy shifted from equity to excellence, and the target level of performance standard was raised from minimum competency to proficiency. Test-driven external accountability has become the linchpin of this policy shift. Despite the policy rhetoric that merges academic excellence and equity, the findings of this book suggest that by far NCLB and state accountability have not worked as originally intended to make adequate progress toward its ambitious goals, that is, achieving high standards for all students and closing the achievement gap. While there can be so many possible reasons to explain this phenomenon of policy failure, we need to carefully assess and counteract existing threats to the validity of test-driven accountability policy from scientific, institutional and technical perspectives:

1. Scientific threats to a test-driven educational accountability system arise when the legitimacy of high-stakes testing policy is threatened by its reliance on limited and possibly biased source of research evidence.

2. Institutional threats arise when top-down policy mandates for achieving unrealistically high performance standards meet school realities in which different professional values, limited instructional capacity and resources undermine the fidelity of policy implementation.

3. Technical threats to an accountability system arise when high-stakes testing faces measurement challenges by which desirable psychometric properties (validity, reliability, and fairness) of testing and accountability measures are lacking and questionable.

BACK TO THE CORE MISSION OF NCLB: CLOSING THE LEARNING GAP VERSUS CLOSING THE TESTING GAP

Can NCLB close the achievement gap by means of closing the testing gap? NCLB may have been successful in disseminating more standardized tests to schools, drawing their attention to test results on the achievement gap, and generating pressure for schools to fix the achievement gap. Before NCLB, not all states participated in the voluntary NAEP state assessment program or administered their own statewide assessments with consequences for their schools and teachers. As a result of NCLB testing requirements, standardized testing has become ubiquitous in all schools across the nation in an effort to narrow the testing gap (more precisely, the high-stakes testing opportunity gap) between the U.S. and other countries with national testing. This brought a Golden Age to the educational testing industry while many low-performing schools and their teachers struggle for survival.

As of today, however, NCLB has been unsuccessful in addressing another kind of testing gap; there are enormous discrepancies between NAEP and state assessment results on students' reading and math proficiency. Before NCLB, the testing gap was an issue in first-generation accountability states such as Texas and Kentucky, which served as a model for the test-driven school accountability system. After NCLB, the same problem may spread to second-generation accountability states such as Connecticut and Maine which did not adopt high-stakes testing until NCLB.

The testing gap arises partly from the contradiction that high-stakes testing serves not only as a measure of outcomes but also as part of the policy intervention. This double-edged role of high-stakes testing, as both intervention and evaluation tools, may lead to a kind of catch-22 for educators. Teachers may have to teach to the test in order to survive this high-stakes testing game, but at the same time their winning means a potential loss for students, since inflated test results may come at the cost of eroding professional decision-making about teaching and impeding genuine progress in student learning. Even at the state level, states now try to win this game under NCLB as they attempt to dodge the bullet by either setting the target low, delaying the progress schedule, negotiating the rules with the U.S. Department of Education, or inventing ways to make their schools look better.[13] This requires careful scrutiny of current state test measures used for accountability and their makeshift strategies that are designed to help prevent massive school failure. Contamination of the test measures will come to threaten the policy as an intervention.

Ultimately, NCLB may be able to fix this kind of testing gap as well. As Congress moves to reauthorize NCLB, it may consider increasing the rigor of state standards and tests by linking them to those set at the national level. Now the central question is whether and how this policy movement toward national standards and testing will contribute to closing the learning gap as much as to closing the testing gap. Despite higher learning expectations for all students, more tightened federal school accountability policy could increase the risk of mandating a level of learning measured by national tests such as NAEP and adding a new layer of high-stakes testing.

The current test-driven accountability system appears to have fallen into the trap of bringing a vicious cycle of more and more testing to futile ends. It is as though patients took medication but did not get satisfactory results at first, so then doctors prescribed an even stronger dose of treatment, ignoring evidence of harmful side effects. While failure is not an option in education, it is important to acknowledge the limitations of the current policy and to find solutions to problems that may have impeded national and state progress toward academic excellence and equity. It is time to reexamine the law, particularly in light of the evidence on the inefficacy of test-driven external accountability policy for equity. This study cannot pinpoint problems that may have impeded national and state progress towards academic excellence and equity. However, in my opinion, NCLB has gone too far in shifting the focus of accountability in an extreme fashion and it is time to restore the balance between inputs and outcomes, between pressure and support for schools, and between educators and other parties in education. Based on the findings of this book, as well as the review of previous studies on accountability issues, the following policy recommendations are made for consideration as we approach the debate about reauthorization of the NCLB.

We need to revise the current policy approach to closing the achievement gap in light of the inefficacy of test-driven external accountability policy under NCLB. This requires more than reducing onerous testing requirements and moving the focus of accountability from testing to teaching and learning. We need to restore the balance between pressure and support for schools by helping particularly low-income, high-minority ones build capacity to teach low-achieving kids. This requires fully funding the mandates and reducing existing educational inequalities.

We need to fully acknowledge that the issues of educational equity occur in many places but not in schools alone. It is true that educational inequity in schools mirrors social inequity but at the same time underlies other inequities in a larger society. There is no single educational policy that can address racial and social inequalities in academic achievement. We need to address a broader range of educational inequity in multiple domains, which involves both schools and social institutions simultaneously.

We also need to redress the current asymmetry of the accountability target and information by reallocating educational responsibilities and information between teachers, parents and any others who are involved in the education of students. Although schools should remain the key unit of accountability, parents need to get more involved in schooling processes and students also need to be held accountable for their learning outcomes, as enlisting student efforts and family support are crucial for school success.

We have to redesign the current incentive system of high-stakes testing by shifting the primary basis of test consequences (rewards/sanctions) from the status of achievement to focus on the progress that school systems make toward the goal. Regardless of the measure and method chosen for setting AYP target and evaluating school progress, the ultimate concern is not simply raising the number of schools meeting their AYP targets in the short term but rather enhancing the schools' capacity for sustained genuine academic improvement over the long haul. Given a limited amount of resources available from the federal government and the limited capacity of the state agencies as well, reducing the identification of schools in need of improvement would help states provide more targeted assistance to a smaller number of disadvantaged schools which have a large number of at-risk students. Nevertheless, applying and modifying the rules of the AYP should not be compromised by future prospects of limited support and short-term interests in reducing school identifications. The long-term success of the school accountability system does not depend on the sheer number of passing schools and students on standardized tests but on the genuine progress of student learning and value-added school performance.

Given the original mission of NCLB, which is closing the achievement gap, any short-term tactical efforts to close the testing gap must not take precedence over long-term strategic efforts to close the learning gap or teaching gap. It may take only a few months to fix the testing gap, but it could take up to several decades to close the learning gap or teaching gap.[14] True war on the achievement gap has just begun.

NOTES

1. The history of education reform has often been depicted as "tinkering toward utopia." (Tyack & Cuban, 1995) or "swinging pendulum" (Kaestle, 1985). Despite these common metaphors, Elmore (2002) points out that in

the history of federal education policy, the disconnect between policy and practice has never been so evident, nor so dangerous, as the current test-driven accountability system as envisioned by NCLB.

2. See previous studies which reported interstate variations in school funding (Carey, 2004), in-field teaching (Jerald, 2002), and student performance standards (Hall & Kennedy, 2006).

3. Although different studies using different methods with data from different states suggested different cost estimates, most revealed needs for massive new investments in education spending; increases in base cost were in the 15–46% range (Mathis, 2003; Rebell, 2006). Studies also suggest that the need for increased funding can be offset partly by reducing inefficiency in current school operations.

4. The next round of NAEP reading and math assessment is slated for 2007, six years since NCLB, and can give a more valid and reliable estimation of the full impact of NCLB. It will not only gives more post-NCLB data points for more reliable assessment of the trends, but will also allow us to investigate pre-to-post NCLB changes in cohort-based gains between grade 4 and grade 8 (1992 to 1996, 1996 to 2000 vs. 2003 to 2007).

5. This proposal simply describes how this new shift in accountability policy may work in theory. It is necessary to investigate the feasibility, trade offs, and the costs of actually implementing such a system. Further, comparative analysis of states in terms of policy shifts is in order. Some states are likely to be farther along in making progress toward the new system than others.

6. Some claim that accountability policy should involve consequences for individual students so that schools and teachers can have the leverage to effectively change student behaviors and improve their achievement (Bishop, 2001; Peterson, 2006; Porter & Chester, 2002). It is true that NCLB lacks the balance of school vs. school accountability. As with school accountability, the idea of enhancing student accountability also should involve efforts to put internal accountability mechanism in place before pushes for external accountability by improving students' intrinsic rather than extrinsic motivation for learning.

7. Parent involvement in children's education is one of the most important strategies for improving students' academic achievement (Epstein, Herrick, & Coates, 1996). The importance of parental involvement is also emphasized by NCLB, which includes important provisions for engaging families. Many have come to realize that schools alone cannot meet NCLB's goal of closing the achievement gap, and acknowledge that multiple sources of influences beyond the classroom (families, community-based organizations and youth service agencies that provide out-of-school complementary learning) are critical to improve achievement outcomes (Weiss, 2005).

8. See Sunderman et al. (2005). If districts in need of improvement are allowed to serve as supplemental educational service providers, they may compete with private centers or community organizations for enhanced accountability.

9. Syntheses of a large body of research, "education production function" studies, provided mixed evidence on the effects of educational expenditures on student achievement (Hanushek, 1997; Hedges, Laine, & Greenwald, 1994). Hanushek (1994) argued that the lack of a systematic relationship between school resources and student achievement makes a

definition of "adequacy" in funding and resources virtually impossible. However, some studies documented significant effects of school resources such as instructional spending and well-qualified teachers on academic achievement (Ferguson, 1991; Ferguson & Ladd, 1996).

10. See Clotfleter, Ladd, Vigor, and Aliaga (2004) and Sunderman et al. (2005).

11. The history of NAEP evolution suggests its possible use for school-level evaluation in the future; in fact, NAEP has expanded its target unit of assessment and reporting with an increasing degree of disaggregation over the past 30 years, starting from a nation-level assessment, adding state-level assessment and most recently adding district-level assessment.

12. A similar suggestion along with the use of scale score rather than percent proficient was made by other analysts (Linn et al., 2002). While using an effect size metric with scale scores may help set more realistic performance targets and better recognize schools' academic progress, it is not permissible under the current law. This idea also raises questions as to whether to use standard deviation of student-level test scores or school-level average test scores and whether to derive the standard deviation from original test score variance or residual variance with adjustments for demographic differences among students and their schools. In Maine and Kentucky, the school-level standard deviation was only 40 percent of the student-level standard deviation of mathematics achievement scores. Once the differences among schools in their students' racial and socioeconomic background characteristics, the adjusted school-level variance of residuals is reduced further down to the half of original school-level variance (see Lee & Coladarci, 2002 for the analysis of within-school vs. between-school math achievement distributions in Maine and Kentucky).

13. Since states are permitted to shape schedules of improvement flexibly under NCLB, many states including Kentucky and Maine adopted a stair-step approach that would allow schools to improve slowly in the first few years as improvements are phased in, and then more dramatically once improvements are fully implemented (see Kentucky Department of Education, 2004; Maine Department of Education, 2003). Although this kind of procrastination approach may help schools earn time to develop capacity, the delay will have ripple effects on later chances of meeting the target.

14. Given setbacks in national progress toward closing racial achievement gaps in the 1990s, it is not clear whether the experience of the past decade is the exception or the rule (see Lee, 2002; Peterson, 2006). Peterson (2006) argues that the task of closing the gap could have been accomplished without the setback, and that past enormous gains can be repeated within the next generation or so. While the optimism of closing the gap is often based on the theory of intergenerational transfer of human capital, there are also negative social trends such as school resegregation (Orfield & Yun, 1999) and deterioration of social capital (Putnam, 1995) that could work against narrowing of the gap. Further, policy assurance of rosy future becomes more challenging as the goal upgraded to closing the gap at more advanced knowledge and at a higher-order skills level. Despite the apparent progress in readily available measures of school quality, disparities remain in less observable but more crucial measures of quality such as teacher knowledge and skills (see Ingersoll, 1996; Lee, 2004c).

PART IV

APPENDICES

APPENDIX A

MEASURES OF STATE ACCOUNTABILITY

State Activism in Test-Driven External Accountability

This book utilizes the measures of test-driven external accountability policy for 50 states as constructed by Lee and Wong (2004). It is based on survey data collected in the mid to late 1990s from three sources: (1) 1995-96 data from the North Central Regional Education Laboratory (NCREL) and Council of Chief State School Officers (CCSSO) (NCREL/CCSSO, 1996), (2) 1999 data from Quality Counts (QC) report (Education Week, 1999), and (3) 1999-2000 data from the Consortium for Policy Research in Education (CPRE) report (Goertz & Duffy, 2002). The NCREL/CCSSO survey covers student assessments, student accountability (testing for promotion, awards/recognition, and graduation), teacher accountability (certification gain/loss, financial rewards/penalties, probation), and school accountability (funding gain/loss, accreditation loss, awards/recognition, performance reporting, probation/warning, takeover/dissolution). The QC survey covers only student assessments and school accountability (report cards, ratings, rewards, assistance and sanctions). The CPRE survey covers student assessments and student and school accountability policies (school/district sanctions or rewards, high school exit test).

Here are some sample questions and response options from the NCREL/CCSSO survey:

The Testing Gap, pages 123–126
147

1. *What uses are made of the results of the assessment for student accountability?*
   (1) Student awards or recognition, (2) Promotion, (3) Honors diploma, (4) Endorsed diploma, (5) Graduation.
2. *What uses are made of the results of the assessment for school accountability?*
   (1) School awards or recognition, (2) School performance reporting, (3) High school skills guarantee, (4) School accreditation.
3. *Does this assessment have consequences for schools?*
   (1) Funding gain, (2) Exemption from regulations, (3) Warnings, (4) Probation, watch lists, (5) Funding loss, (6) Accreditation loss, (7) Takeover, (8) Dissolution.
4. *Does this assessment have consequences for school staff?*
   (1) Financial rewards, (2) Certification status gain, (3) Probation, (4) Certification status loss, (5) Financial penalties.

Policy index scores were calculated for each state by summing the number of policies adopted and in place by the state at the time of survey. The NCREL/CCSSO policy index ranges from zero to 16 (M = 6.5, SD = 4.2). The reliability of this 26-item 1995 NCREL/CCSSO accountability policy index is very high (alpha = .85). The QC policy index ranges from zero to 6 (M = 3.0, SD = 1.8). The reliability of this 6-item 1999 QC accountability policy index is high (alpha = .77). Finally, the CPRE policy index was constructed by Carnoy and Loeb (2002) and it ranges from zero to five (M = 2.1, SD = 1.4).

The 1995 NCREL/CCSSO policy index is moderately correlated with the other measures from more recent surveys of accountability policies, including the 2000 CPRE accountability index (r = .59) and the 1999 Quality Counts accountability index (r =.63). The correlation between CPRE and QC policy indices is also similar (r = .61). Despite the moderate correlations among three policy indices, the stronger evidence of convergent validity is shown when the comparison is made for common items: (1) performance reporting, (2) awards/recognition/rewards, and (3) takeover/dissolution/reconstitution. For these 50 states' three major school accountability policies, CPRE and Quality Counts reports are almost perfectly consistent with each other, and NCREL/CCSSO report shows only moderate degree of agreement. Discrepancies between the NCREL/CCSSO and the two other reports may be attributed to the time interval between the two surveys and possible policy changes in the interim period.

Out of these three related policy measures, Lee and Wong (2004) created a composite factor of state activism in test-driven external accountability policy during the 1990s. One factor is retained through principal component analysis of the three state-level policy index variables with high factor loadings: '95 NCREL/CCSSO policy index, .85; '99 Quality

Counts policy index, .87; and 2000 CPRE policy index, .85. Factor analysis is a technique for data reduction with extraction of principal components (underlying factors) from multiple variables. By examining a set of variables with high factor loadings on the same factor, we can interpret the meaning of identified factor. In this case, all three variables used tap into the same construct and they are almost equally weighted to produce a composite factor; it has an eigen value of 2.2 and explains 74 percent of the combined variance. Table A.1 shows the factor scores of this policy construct, "state activism in test-driven external accountability" for all fifty states. The factor scores are standardized to have a mean of zero and a standard deviation of one.

TABLE A.1
Measures of State Accountability

State	Test-Driven External Accountability Factor Score	Component Scores		
		NCREL/ CCSSO	Quality Counts	CPRE
Alabama	1.34	11	5	4
Alaska	−0.85	3	2	1
Arizona	−0.58	3	2	2
Arkansas	−0.79	6	1	1
California	0.04	4	2	4
Colorado	−1.34	0	1	1
Connecticut	−0.48	7	2	1
Delaware	−0.94	2	2	1
Florida	1.05	5	5	5
Georgia	0.10	8	3	2
Hawaii	−0.66	5	2	1
Idaho	−1.07	3	1	1
Illinois	0.85	10	5	3
Indiana	1.01	8	6	3
Iowa	−1.82	0	0	0
Kansas	0.08	6	5	1
Kentucky	1.61	14	5	4
Louisiana	1.07	11	5	3
Maine	−0.79	6	1	1
Maryland	1.83	14	6	4
Massachusetts	−0.86	0	2	2
Michigan	0.82	14	5	1
Minnesota	−0.49	4	2	2
Mississippi	0.02	9	1	3

(continued)

TABLE A.1
Measures of State Accountability (continued)

State	Test-Driven External Accountability Factor Score	Component Scores		
		NCREL/ CCSSO	Quality Counts	CPRE
Missouri	−0.35	7	2	2
Montana	−0.97	4	1	1
Nebraska	−1.82	0	0	0
Nevada	0.12	5	5	2
New Hampshire	−1.07	3	1	1
New Jersey	0.98	9	3	5
New Mexico	1.28	8	6	4
New York	1.51	10	5	5
North Carolina	2.01	13	6	5
North Dakota	−0.79	6	1	1
Ohio	0.05	7	2	3
Oklahoma	0.54	11	5	1
Oregon	−0.45	3	2	3
Pennsylvania	−0.63	3	3	1
Rhode Island	−0.63	3	3	1
South Carolina	0.82	13	3	3
South Dakota	−0.76	4	2	1
Tennessee	0.20	13	2	2
Texas	2.28	16	6	5
Utah	−0.57	6	2	1
Vermont	−0.29	2	5	1
Virginia	0.31	8	4	2
Washington	−0.57	6	2	1
West Virginia	0.71	8	4	4
Wisconsin	0.04	5	4	2
Wyoming	−1.12	0	2	1

APPENDIX B

Summary of Cross-State Causal-Comparative and Correlational Studies on the Effects of High-Stakes Testing and Accountability Policies on Academic Achievement

Studies	Independent Variables (Policy)	Dependent Variables (Achievement)	Samples	Analytic Methods	Effect Sizes (Standardized Group Mean Differences)
Frederiksen (1994)	Minimum competency testing	NAEP 1978–1986 math scores	9-year, 13-year, and 17-year old students in 25–28 states (classified into 3 groups as high-stakes, moderate, and low-stakes states)	Age-based analysis of math gain scores in high-stakes vs. low-stakes states	Positive (small)[a] .22 for 9-year math routine .13 for 9-year math nonroutine .08 13-year math routine .12 for 13-year math nonroutine .02 for 17-year math routine .05 for 17-year math nonroutine
Lee (1998b)	Standards-based education reform including high-stakes testing policies in the 1980s	NAEP 1992 math scores	4th and 8th graders in 40 states	Cross-sectional analysis of the relationship between state policy and achievement	Negative (small)[b] –.33 for grade 4 math –.46 for grade 8 math
Grissmer & Flanagan (1998)	Standards-based assessments and school accountability system adopted in the 1980s and 1990s	NAEP 1990–96 math, 1992–94 reading scores	4th and 8th graders in North Carolina and Texas vs. the average state	Case study (indirect estimation of policy effects on gain scores as unexplained by changes in student and school factors)	Positive (small)[c] .22 for 90–96 8th math .25 for 92–96 4th math .07 for 92–94 4th reading

(continued)

APPENDIX B
Summary of Cross-State Causal-Comparative and Correlational Studies on the Effects of High-Stakes Testing and Accountability Policies on Academic Achievement (continued)

Studies	Independent Variables (Policy)	Dependent Variables (Achievement)	Samples	Analytic Methods	Effect Sizes (Standardized Group Mean Differences)
Bishop et al. (2001)	School accountability (stakes for schools and teachers), Minimum competency exam (MCE), End-of-course exam (EOCE)	NAEP 1998 reading, 1996 math scores	4th and 8th graders in 35–43 states (comparing New York and North Carolina with EOCE/MCE with others)	Cross-sectional analysis of three types of accountability policy effects with control for state demographic background variables	Positive for school accountability (small)[d] .49 for '98 4th reading .22 for '98 8th reading .27 for '96 4th math .13 for '96 8th math Insignificant for MCE .00 for '98 4th reading .14 for '98 8th reading .33 for '96 4th math .04 for '96 8th math Positive for EOCE/MCE (medium to large) .79 for '98 4th reading 1.24 for '98 8th reading 1.20 for '96 4th math .54 for '96 8th math

Study	Policy	Data	Analysis	Results
Jacob (2001)	High school graduation exams (minimum competency tests) adopted in the late 1970s and 1980s	NELS 1988–1992 reading and math scores	Longitudinal analysis of student achievement gains (with controls for student, school and state characteristics)	Insignificant[c] .04 for '88 8th–'92 12th math .001 for '88 8th–'92 12th reading
Amrein & Berliner (2002)	Index of high-stakes testing policies adopted in the 1970s–1990s including graduation exams, public report cards, rewards or sanctions	NAEP 1992–2000 math, 1990–2000 math, 1992–1998 reading scores	Grade-based and cohort-based analyses of relative gain scores (as deviations from the national average gain scores)	Mixed (small)[f] .35 for '92–'00 4th math .14 for '90–'00 8th math .28 for '92–'98 4th reading –.38 for '96 4th–'00 8th math .02 for '94 4th–'98 8th reading
Carnoy & Loeb (2002)	External accountability policy index (5 point scale), including high school exit exam, school report cards, rewards and sanctions as of 1999–2000	NAEP 1996–2000 math achievement levels (Basic and Proficient)	Grade-based analysis of gains in percent Basic by racial group (adjustment for baseline achievement, demographics, per pupil revenue, and changes in the population)	Positive (small to large)[g] .10 for '96–'00 4th White .77 for '96–'00 4th Black .54 for '96–'00 4th Hispanic .78 for '96–'00 8th White .95 for '96–'00 8th Black 1.04 for '96–'00 8th Hispanic

(continued)

APPENDIX B

Summary of Cross-State Causal-Comparative and Correlational Studies on the Effects of High-Stakes Testing and Accountability Policies on Academic Achievement (continued)

Studies	Independent Variables (Policy)	Dependent Variables (Achievement)	Samples	Analytic Methods	Effect Sizes (Standardized Group Mean Differences)
Raymond & Hanushek (2003)	1. Amrein & Berliner's list of high-stakes testing states 2. Authors' own classification of states' school accountability systems	NAEP 1992–2000 and 1996–2000 math scores	4th and 8th graders in 34–36 states	Grade-based and cohort-based analysis of gain scores (adjustment for changes in exclusion rates, spending on education, parents' education)	Positive (large)[h] 1.16 for '92–'00 4th math .71 for '96–'00 4th math .79 for '92–'00 8th math .74 for '96–'00 8th math .83 for '96 4th–'00 8th math
Rosenshine (2003)	Amrein & Berliner's list of "clear" high-stakes testing states, excluding states with changing exclusion rates	NAEP 1996–2000 math, 1994–1998 reading scores	4th and 8th graders in 20–26 states	Grade-based analysis of state average gain scores	Positive (small to moderate)[i] .35 for '96–'00 4th grade math .79 for '96–'00 8th grade math .62 for '94–'98 4th grade reading
Amrein-Beardsely & Berliner (2003)	"Clear" high-stakes testing states (excluding "unclear" states with increased exclusion rates)	NAEP 1996–2000 math, 1994–1998 reading scores	4th and 8th graders in 12–16 states	Grade-based descriptive analysis of state average gain scores	Mixed (small to large)[j] 1.2 for '96–'00 4th grade math .77 for '96–'00 8th grade math −.33 for '94–'98 4th grade reading

Braun (2004)	Amrein & Berliner's list of high-stakes testing states	NAEP 1992–2000 math scores	4th and 8th graders in 33 states	Grade-based and cohort-based analyses of relative gain scores (as deviations from the national average)	Mixed (small to large)[k] .96 for '92–'00 4th grade math .81 for '92–'00 8th grade math –.67 for '92 4th–'96 8th grade math –.31 for '96 4th–'00 8th grade math
Lee & Wong (2004)	A composite factor of state activism in test-driven accountability policy during the 1990s	NAEP 1992–2000 math scores	8th graders in 31 states	Grade-based trend analysis of gain scores (adjusted for baseline status, demographics, schooling conditions)	Positive (small)[l] .28 for '92–'00 grade 8th All .27 for '92–'00 8th White .39 for '92–'00 8th Black .18 for '92–'00 8th Hispanic

Notes:

[a] The effect size was estimated with information from the original study by dividing high-stakes vs. low-stakes state average gain score differences by the standard deviations of student test scores.

[b] The effect size was estimated with information from the original study by converting the correlations between state policy activism and state average math achievement into standardized group mean differences.

[c] The effect size was estimated with information from the original study by subtracting the average standardized gain scores of the two states (North Carolina and Texas) from the average of all states' standardized gain scores.

[d] The effect size was estimated with information from the original study by dividing the regression coefficients for respective policies by the standard deviations of test scores.

[e] The effect size was estimated with information from the original study by dividing the OLS regression coefficients for graduation test by the standard deviations of 12th grade scores.

(continued)

APPENDIX B
Summary of Cross-State Causal-Comparative and Correlational Studies on the Effects of High-Stakes Testing and Accountability Policies on Academic Achievement (continued)

f The effect size was estimated with information from the original study by dividing the state average gain scores of 18 high-stakes states (as deviations from the national average gain scores) by their standard deviations. Among the 18 high-stakes states identified by the study, 10 states had available data for 1990–2000 8th grade gain, 13 states for 1992–2000 4th grade gain, and 13 states for 1992–1998 4th grade reading gain.

g The effect size was estimated with information from the original study in which a two-step move in the accountability (e.g., from 1 to 3) was associated with gain scores. The regression coefficient for accountability policy (change in the gain score with one unit increase in accountability policy) was multiplied by 2 to estimate the average difference between weak and strong accountability states. Then, the effect size was obtained by dividing the average gain score difference by the standard deviation of state gain scores.

h The effect size was estimated with information from the original study. The effect size for their re-analysis of Amrein and Berliner's study was obtained by dividing the average difference between high-stakes states and non-accountability states (high stakes advantage after adjusting for changes in students excluded from NAEP) by corresponding standard deviations of state gain scores. The effect size for the study's own analysis of school accountability policy was obtained by transforming the percentage gain difference between states with and without accountability systems into logit.

i The effect size was reported by the original study. It was obtained by dividing the state average gain score difference between Amrein and Berliner's clear high-stakes states and other states by the standard deviations of gain scores.

j The effect size was estimated with information from the original study by dividing the state average gain score difference between their newly identified list of clear high-stakes states and other states by the standard deviations of gain scores.

k The effect size was estimated with information from the original study by dividing the state average gain score difference between high-stakes and low-stakes testing states by the standard deviations of gain scores.

l The effect size was estimated with information from the original study. The regression coefficients for accountability policy, the estimates of yearly average gain with one standard deviation increase in accountability factor score during the 1992–2000 period, were multiplied by 16 to obtain estimates of cumulative policy effect over the 8-year period between strong vs. weak accountability states (2 standard deviation differences from the mean). Then the cumulative policy effect was divided by the standard deviation of test scores. The effect size for each racial group was estimated in the same ways.

DESCRIPTION OF SCHOOL ORGANIZATIONAL CONTEXT VARIABLES

1. ORGANIZATIONAL VALUES (PRIORITY OF EDUCATIONAL GOALS)

The following variables are constructed from 1993–94 SASS public school administrator survey data. Public school principals in each state were asked to choose from a list of educational goals those they felt were most important, second most important, and third most important.

Basic Skills: Percentage of principals giving the highest priorities (most important educational goal) to basic literacy skills (reading, math, writing, speaking).

Academic Excellence: Percentage of principals giving the highest priorities (most important educational goal) to academic excellence.

Personal Growth: Percentage of principals giving the highest priorities (most important educational goal) to personal growth (self-esteem, self-knowledge, and so on).

Human Relations: Percentage of principals giving the highest priorities (most important educational goal) to human relations.

The Testing Gap, pages 133–135
Copyright © 2007 by Information Age Publishing

2. ORGANIZATIONAL POWER
(LOCUS OF EDUCATIONAL CONTROL)

The following variables are constructed from 1993–94 SASS public school administrator survey data. Principals were asked to rate the influence of various groups, including state department of education, school board, principals, teachers and parents, regarding key decisions such as school curriculum and hiring teachers on a 6-point scale of influence (6 representing a great deal of influence).

Principal Influence on Curriculum: Percentage of principals who report that "principals" have a great deal of influence on establishing the school curriculum.

Teacher Influence on Curriculum: Percentage of principals who report that "teachers" have a great deal of influence on establishing the school curriculum.

Principal Influence on Hiring Teachers: Percentage of principals who report that "principals" have a great deal of influence on hiring full-time teachers.

Teacher Influence on Hiring Teachers: Percentage of principals who report that "teachers" have a great deal of influence on hiring full-time teachers.

3. ORGANIZATIONAL CLIMATE AND CAPACITY
(QUALITY OF TEACHING CONDITIONS)

The following variables are constructed from 1996 NAEP school principal survey data or 1993–94 SASS public school teacher survey data.

Safe/Orderly Climate: Seven items from the 1996 NAEP school principal survey were used to "measure" safe/orderly climate. The questions ask how serious problems schools have in terms of safety, student behaviors, and orderliness. Applying the Rasch model to those seven 4-point item responses for a composite measure of safe/orderly climate produced item separation reliability of .99 and person separation reliability (an equivalent of alpha) of .79.

Collective Support: Seven items from the 1996 NAEP school principal survey were used to "measure" collective support. The questions ask whether school community members (teachers, students and parents) have positive relations with each other and also have positive attitudes toward and support for academic learning. Applying the Rasch model to those seven 4-point item responses for a composite measure collective support produced item separation reliability of .98 and person separation reliability (an equivalent of alpha) of .75.

Teacher Commitment (Plan to Remain in Teaching): Percentage of public school teachers who report that they plan to remain in teaching while they are able. The variable was derived from the 1993–94 SASS public school teacher survey data.

Teacher Qualification (In-Field Teaching): Percentage of public school secondary teachers in core subjects (English, math, science, social studies) who have a major in the subject area they teach. The variable was derived from the 1993-94 SASS public school teacher survey data.

DESCRIPTION OF MAINE SCHOOL PROFILE VARIABLES USED IN MEA SCHOOL PERFORMANCE STATUS AND PROGRESS ANALYSIS

Variable	Description	Source
School Size	Total number of students enrolled in school	School student file for 1995
Pupil-Teacher Ratio	Number of students divided by number of teachers in school	School staff file and student file for 1995
Per Pupil Expenditures	Local district expenditures for average resident pupil on regular programs of study. Excluding expenditures on vocational and special education.	District expenditure file for FY 1995
School Poverty	Percentage of students eligible for free or reduced lunch in school	School student file for 1995
Teacher Education	Percentage of teachers in school who hold master's degree or plus some advanced, or Ph.D.	School staff file for 1995
Teaching Experience	Average of teachers' years of teaching in school	School staff file for 1995

(continued)

The Testing Gap, pages 137–138
Copyright © 2007 by Information Age Publishing

Variable	Description	Source
Adequacy of Instructional Materials	Average of school principals' responses over the survey questions about the availability and adequacy of textbooks, other print materials, instructional supplies, and computer software. The rating scale involves 3-point response: 1 (inadequate), 2 (adequate), and 3 (excellent).	1994 Maine Public School Census file
Adequacy of Instructional Equipment	Average of school principals' responses over the survey questions about the availability and adequacy of TVs/VCRs, camcorders, overhead projectors, slide projectors, CD players, CD ROM units, filmstrip projectors, record players, still cameras, computers, video disk players, LCD plates. The rating scale involves 4-point response: 1 (none), 2 (inadequate), 3 (adequate), and 4 (excellent).	1994 Maine Public School Census file

APPENDIX E

DATA AND STATISTICAL METHODS FOR TREND ANALYSIS

DATA

NAEP provides repeated cross-sectional measures of reading and math achievement for each grade. The NAEP results are reported in two ways: scale scores and the percentages of students scoring at or above three benchmarks called achievement levels (Perie, Grigg, & Donahue, 2005 for reading; Perie, Grigg, & Dion, 2005 for math). NAEP reading and math scores are on a 0-500 scale. Interpretation of the NAEP scale scores is made with reference to performance standards for each subject and grade, using corresponding cut scores for three achievement levels: Basic, Proficient and Advanced.

This study used national-level and state-level aggregate measures of performance in scale scores and the percentages of students scoring at or above Proficient level that were drawn from 1990-2005 NAEP public school sample grade 4 and grade 8 reading and math assessments (www.nces .ed.gov/nationsreportcard). The NAEP national grade 4 and 8 data were drawn from the NAEP database for the following years: 1992, 1994, 1998, 2000 (grade 4 only), 2002, 2003, 2005 in reading and 1990, 1992, 1996, 2000, 2003, 2005 in math. The NAEP state grade 4 and 8 data were drawn from the NAEP database for the following years: 1992 (grade 4 only), 1994 (grade 4 only), 1998, 2002, 2003, 2005 in reading and 1990 (grade 8 only), 1992, 1996, 2000, 2003 and 2005 in math. Grade 12 was not included in the study due to the lack of available data. The NAEP 2005 national results for

The Testing Gap, pages 139–144

grade 12 were not available at the time of this study so that it was not possible to assess post-NCLB trend at the high school level. There are also no NAEP state assessment data at grade 12 or any other high school grades.

Since 1998 in reading and 1996 in math, testing accommodations (e.g., extended testing time, individual test administration) were provided to students with disabilities and/or English language learners. Therefore, the NAEP results with accommodation permitted were used for the 1998-2005 years in reading and for the 1996–2005 years in math. All prior assessment results were without accommodation. For the sake of keeping track of achievement throughout the 1990s prior to NCLB, all available NAEP data points, including results with and without accommodation, were used. Preliminary analysis for this study attempted to adjust the national or state achievement trends for changes in the accommodation policy but did not detect significant bias in the estimation of pre-NCLB achievement trends.

To analyze the racial achievement gap on NAEP, the average achievement of Black and Hispanic students was compared with the average achievement of White students. Although the NAEP data analysis includes Asian and Pacific Islanders as well, the analysis of racial gaps focused on the achievement of Blacks and Hispanics who have significant gaps relative to their White counterparts. To analyze the socioeconomic achievement gap, comparisons were made between Poor and Nonpoor students as classified by eligibility for free or reduced-price lunch. The NAEP data broken down by this school lunch variable for Poor and Nonpoor students and their achievement gap are not available until 1998 in reading and 1996 in math.

Interpretation of the achievement gap on NAEP can be facilitated by using some sort of effect size metrics. One way to think about the size of the achievement gap is considering how large the gap is relative to the standard deviation of NAEP scores. In order to compute standardized gap scores at grades 4 or grade 8, the gap score can be divided by within-grade standard deviation of student scores. The distributions of student scores at the baseline year across the national public school sample are as follows: M = 215, SD = 36 for 1992 grade 4 reading; M = 258, SD = 36 for 1992 grade 8 reading; M = 212, SD = 32 for 1990 grade 4 math; M = 262, SD = 36 for 1990 grade 8 math. Another way to think about the size of the achievement gap is to consider how large the gap is relative to the average amount of gain score per grade on the NAEP scale (about 10–12 point gain per grade based on the difference between grade 4 and grade 8 average scores).

STATISTICAL METHODS

Weighted Least Squares (WLS) regression was used to analyze the national trends of reading and math scores in Chapter 6 and takes into account the precision of national average scores, gaps, or proficiency rates. Weight was calculated by taking the inverse of standard errors of average scores or proficiency estimates for each group and the gap between groups at each time point. More recent assessments tend to have smaller standard errors. The entire period for which NAEP data is available was divided into two periods, Pre-NCLB (1990–2001) and Post-NCLB (2002–2005). The following two-piece linear growth model postulates a national academic growth trajectory with two temporal predictors of outcome Y. It affords testing whether there was significant increment or decrement to the baseline growth rate after NCLB:

$$Y_t = \pi_0 + \pi_1 (\text{Pre-NCLB})_t + \pi_2 (\text{Post-NCLB})_t + e_t$$

Where

Y_t = the measure of nation's average achievement outcome at year t;

$(\text{Pre-NCLB})_t$ = the number of years elapsed since the first NAEP assessment at year t (0 for 1990, 1 for 1991, ..., 15 for 2005);

$(\text{Post-NCLB})_t$ = the number of years elapsed since the enactment of NCLB at year t (0 for 1990 through 2001, 1 for 2002, 2 for 2003, ..., 4 for 2005);

π_0 = the initial status of achievement;

π_1 = pre-NCLB annual growth rate during the baseline time period (achievement gain per year during 1990–2001);

π_2 = post-NCLB increment or decrement to the baseline pre-NCLB growth rate (change in π_1 during 2002–05);

e_t = a random effect representing the deviation of nation's score from the predicted score based on the model.

Hierarchical linear models (HLM), two-piece linear growth models, were used in Chapter 7 to examine interstate variations in the trends of reading and math achievement over the 1990–2005 period (Raudenbush & Bryk, 2002). Since there were four outcome variables for each group (grade 4 reading, grade 4 math, grade 8 reading, and grade 8 math), 2-level HLM analyses were conducted separately for each outcome variable, using the precision of the outcome variable as weight. At Level 1 (time level), the same two temporal predictors were used to keep track of each state i's outcome variable Y at year t. The level-1 coefficients, including initial status (π_{1i}), pre-NCLB growth rate (π_{1i}) and post-NCLB change in the growth rate (π_{2i}), were assumed to vary randomly among states. Also, the study's assumption of independent errors with constant variance is unlikely to distort the analysis for a short time series. At Level 2 (state level), state activism in test-driven external accountability policy was used as one of the predictors to account for these interstate variations in academic growth patterns (see Appendix B for description of the Accountability variable). Further, HLM latent variable regression method was used to control for the effect of initial status on pre-NCLB gain as well as the effect of both initial status and pre-NCLB growth rate on post-NCLB change.

Level 1 Model:

$$Y_{ti} = \pi_{0i} + \pi_{1i}(\text{Pre-NCLB})_{ti} + \pi_{2i}(\text{Post-NCLB})_{ti} + e_{ti}$$

Level 2 Model:

$$\pi_{0i} = \beta_{00} + \beta_{01}(\text{Accountability})_i + r_{0i}$$
$$\pi_{1i} = \beta_{10} + \beta_{11}(\text{Accountability})_i + \beta_{12}(\pi_{0i}) + r_{1i}$$
$$\pi_{2i} = \beta_{20} + \beta_{21}(\text{Accountability})_i + \beta_{22}(\pi_{0i}) + \beta_{23}(\pi_{1i}) + r_{2i}$$

It needs to be noted that the above growth model is simply one of several possible models since there are other alternative growth models (Singer & Willet, 2003). The above model postulates a discontinuity in slope, not elevation; it is hypothesized that the growth rate changes after NCLB. In contrast, a model can include a discontinuity in elevation, not slope; it means that a temporary change right after NCLB is followed by a return to the pre-reform growth rate. This alternative model was also tested separately and the results from grade 4 reading and math only provided limited support for the model with the NAEP average grade 4 reading scores for All, White, Nonpoor and grade 4 math scores for Black and Hispanic. Testing a model with a discontinuity in both elevation and slope together was not possible due to insufficient post-NCLB data points.

One advantage of the multilevel model for change is that it improves the precision of estimation of individual growth parameters. These model-based estimates of growth trajectories combine Ordinary Least Squares (OLS) estimates with population average estimates derived from the fitted models. This combination yields a superior, more precise, estimate when data are sparse. For instance, in this study, there may be too few data points in some states to enable valid statistical inferences on the average proficiency or gap trend using traditional regression models. HLM models can use not only the data in those short-term states but also information in the pooled data for all states, including long-term ones. Therefore, the pooling involved in multilevel models affords a "borrowing of strength" that supports statistical inference in a situation where no inference would be possible using traditional methods (Raudenbush & Bryk, 2002; Singer & Willet, 2003). This HLM analysis provided for testing statistical significance of the growth rate in each state. Statistical significance of each state's pre-NCLB growth and post-NCLB change was determined by using a more rigorous alpha level of .001, which controls for familywise Type I errors in testing the same set of hypotheses with all 50 states.

It needs to be noted that this study involved tracking successive cohort groups of students at the same grade over time. This grade-based (repeated cross-sectional) comparison method that tracks test score changes for the same grade (e.g., 1996 8th grade to 2000 8th grade) contrasts with a cohort-based (quasi-longitudinal) comparison method which tracks the performance of the same cohort group (e.g., 1996 4th grade to 2000 8th grade). Review of previous studies on the impact of accountability on achievement revealed contradictory results between the two methods; the grade-based comparison method tended to produce more positive results whereas the cohort-based comparison method showed more negative effects (see Chapter 2, this volume). Examination of the post-NCLB achievement trend through the cohort-based method is not possible yet, since the currently available post-NCLB NAEP data does not afford a 4-year interval between the measures.

Another potential factor that may confound the results of the average achievement and gap trend analysis is change in the identification and exclusion of certain groups of students for NAEP testing, particularly students with learning disabilities (SWD) and English language learners (ELL). Increasing number of ELL students particularly among Hispanic and Asian immigrant populations, could have influenced the average Hispanic and Asian achievement trends. On one hand, as a result of demographic changes, the national average identification rate of SWD and/or ELL students in NAEP has increased over the past 15 years and thus tends to be higher for the post-NCLB period than for the pre-NCLB period. On the other hand, as a result of accommodation permitted since 1996 in math and since 1998 in reading, the national average exclusion rate of SWD and/or ELL students in NAEP has decreased over time and thus tends to be somewhat lower for post-NCLB period than for pre-NCLB period. Preliminary analysis of this study showed that these factors do not significantly affect findings on the national trends of reading and math achievement during the post-NCLB period.

Since the exclusion rate of SWD and/or ELL students varied from state to state, we also need to consider this interstate variation for a fair comparison of the state achievement trends. Amrein and Berliner (2002) point out that the larger achievement gains in high-stakes testing states such as North Carolina and Texas are attributable partly to their relatively large increases in exclusion rates. However, Braun (2004) showed that those two states are outliers that deviate from the pattern of weak or no relationship between change in exclusion rate and gain scores among all participating NAEP states. Carnoy and Loeb (2002), Raymond and Haushek (2003), and

Hanushek and Raymond (2004) studies also show that statistically adjusting gain scores for changes in exclusion rates did not lead to significant changes in the estimation of accountability policy effects. Preliminary analysis of this study also did not find significant influence of exclusion rates on state accountability policy effect estimates.

HLM ANALYSIS OF THE RELATIONSHIP BETWEEN STATE ACCOUNTABILITY POLICIES AND STUDENT ACHIEVEMENT OUTCOMES

TABLE F.1
HLM Estimates of State Accountability Policy Effects on NAEP Grade 4 Reading and Math Trends (N = 50 states)

		Reading		Math	
Group	Adjustment	Effect on Pre-NCLB Growth	Effect on Post-NCLB Change	Effect on Pre-NCLB Growth	Effect on Post-NCLB Change
All	Unadjusted	.11	−.13	.26**	−.45**
	Adjusted	.07	−.32	.20*	−.55
White	Unadjusted	.17**	−.43**	.21**	−.41**
	Adjusted	.14*	−.53*	.19**	−.51
Black	Unadjusted	−.11	.46	.06	−.16
	Adjusted	−.12	.43	.06	−.13
Hispanic	Unadjusted	.09	−.15	.08	−.17
	Adjusted	.10	−.01	.15	−.02

(continued)

The Testing Gap, pages 145–147

TABLE F.1
HLM Estimates of State Accountability Policy Effects on NAEP Grade 4 Reading and Math Trends (N = 50 states) (continued)

		Reading		Math	
Group	Adjustment	Effect on Pre-NCLB Growth	Effect on Post-NCLB Change	Effect on Pre-NCLB Growth	Effect on Post-NCLB Change
Asian	Unadjusted	−.03	−.39	.22	−.65
	Adjusted	.14	−.65	.46*	.05
Nonpoor	Unadjusted	−.04	−.06	.04	−.05
	Adjusted	−.01	−.09	.03	−.09
Poor	Unadjusted	.04	−.04	.34*	−.54*
	Adjusted	−.13	−.02	.15	−.41
White–Black	Unadjusted	.20	−.83*	−.02	.09
gap	Adjusted	.21*	−.01	−.03	.06
White–Hispanic	Unadjusted	−.03	−.18	−.11	.10
gap	Adjusted	−.02	−.19	−.11	.30
Poverty gap	Unadjusted	−.10	−.02	−.28**	.41*
	Adjusted	.11	−.10	−.06	0.0

Note. Numbers in "unadjusted" rows show estimated effects of state accountability policy without any statistical control for other covariates. Numbers in "adjusted" rows show estimated effects of state accountability policy with statistical control for initial status and pre-NCLB growth rate. Asterisks indicate statistical significance level of the estimate: * $p < .05$; ** $p < .01$

TABLE F.2
HLM Estimates of State Accountability Policy Effects on NAEP Grade 8 Reading and Math Trends (N = 50 states)

		Reading		Math	
Group	Adjustment	Effect on Pre-NCLB Growth	Effect on Post-NCLB Change	Effect on Pre-NCLB Growth	Effect on Post-NCLB Change
All	Unadjusted	−.12	−.17	.23**	−.14
	Adjusted	−.13	−.28**	.21**	−.15
White	Unadjusted	.05	−.39	.25**	−.27
	Adjusted	.04	−.31**	.20**	−.05
Black	Unadjusted	−.08	−.27	.07	.33
	Adjusted	.02	−.37	.08	.50
Hispanic	Unadjusted	−.44	.25	.56**	−1.23**
	Adjusted	.16	−.35	.35**	−.28

TABLE F.2
HLM Estimates of State Accountability Policy Effects on NAEP Grade 8 Reading and Math Trends (N = 50 states) (continued)

		Reading		Math	
Group	Adjustment	Effect on Pre-NCLB Growth	Effect on Post-NCLB Change	Effect on Pre-NCLB Growth	Effect on Post-NCLB Change
Asian	Unadjusted	−.94	1.27	−.44*	.73
	Adjusted	.29	.27	−.39	−.25
Nonpoor	Unadjusted	.01	−.30	.26*	−.20
	Adjusted	−.01	−.29**	.13	−.15
Poor	Unadjusted	−.24	.15	.59***	−.60*
	Adjusted	−.15	−.18	.18	−.17
White–Black gap	Unadjusted	.15	−.12	.10	−.68*
	Adjusted	.05	.10	.09	−.41*
White–Hispanic gap	Unadjusted	.34	−.47	−.35*	.96**
	Adjusted	−.02	−.02	−.28**	.45
Poverty gap	Unadjusted	.23	−.42	−.40**	.47
	Adjusted	.16	−.07	.04	−.29

Note. Numbers in "unadjusted" rows show estimated effects of state accountability policy without any statistical control for other covariates. Numbers in "adjusted" rows show estimated effects of state accountability policy with statistical control for initial status and pre-NCLB growth rate. Asterisks indicate statistical significance level of the estimate: * $p < .05$; ** $p < .01$; *** $p < .001$.

APPENDIX G

COMPARISON OF NAEP AND STATE ASSESSMENT IN READING AND MATH PROFICIENCY

The NAEP assessment results for individual states were compared with states' own assessment results in 4th and 8th grade reading and math. Since state assessment results were most readily available in the form of the percentage of students who meet a desired standard (typically at or above a Proficient level), proficiency rate data were obtained from each of the 43 state education departments that made this data available on their websites and were matched to corresponding NAEP proficiency rates in the same subject and grade during the same testing year. When all the available data are stacked across multiple years and states, the numbers of maximum data points are as follows: N = 90 in grade 4 math, N = 115 in grade 4 reading, N = 103 in grade 8 reading, N = 82 in grade 8 math. The number of states varies by year: in grade 4 math for example, N = 3 in 1996, N = 17 in 2000, N = 45 in 2003, N = 25 in 2005.

Table G.1 shows the measures of NAEP vs. state assessment discrepancies in each grade and subject across years for 43 states that have both NAEP and state assessment results available. The discrepancy between the two assessments was measured by the ratio of the state assessment-based proficiency rate to the NAEP-based proficiency rate. The more this ratio departs from the value of one, the greater the discrepancies between the

The Testing Gap, pages 149–152
Copyright © 2007 by Information Age Publishing
173

two assessments. A ratio exceeding 1 implies a relatively lower state standard in comparison with the NAEP standard, whereas a ratio falling below 1 implies a relatively higher state standard.

TABLE G.1
Measures of State Accountability and NAEP vs. State Assessment Discrepancies in Reading and Math Proficiency

| | Ratio of State Assessment to NAEP Proficiency | | | |
| | Grade 4 | | Grade 8 | |
State	Reading	Math	Reading	Math
Alabama	—	—	—	—
Alaska	2.78	2.31	2.8	2.13
Arizona	2.71	2.09	2.52	1.44
Arkansas	—	—	—	—
California	1.94	1.79	1.61	1.14
Colorado	2.38	2.42	2.54	2.16
Connecticut	1.6	2.3	2.08	2.27
Delaware	2.44	2.21	2.43	1.79
Florida	1.96	1.74	1.68	2.43
Georgia	3.04	2.96	3.17	3.02
Hawaii	2.25	0.9	1.92	1.05
Idaho	2.56	2.37	2.43	2.1
Illinois	1.94	2.44	1.83	1.82
Indiana	2.29	2	2.13	2.35
Iowa	2.19	2.14	1.93	2.19
Kansas	2.12	1.92	2	1.79
Kentucky	2.02	1.73	1.71	1.29
Louisiana	3	2.93	2.35	3.41
Maine	1.43	0.94	1.17	0.77
Maryland	1.62	1.95	1.43	1.68
Massachusetts	1.23	0.9	1.56	0.94
Michigan	2.45	1.92	2.26	2
Minnesota	1.88	1.83	—	—
Mississippi	5.01	4.26	2.76	3.89
Missouri	1.05	1.41	0.99	0.55
Montana	2.16	2.42	1.93	2
Nebraska	—	—	—	—
Nevada	2.2	2.06	2.31	2.38
New Hampshire	1.91	1.84	—	—
New Jersey	2.06	1.65	1.94	1.72
New Mexico	2.37	3	2.55	3
New York	1.81	2.73	1.33	1.59
North Carolina	2.58	2.63	2.96	2.6
North Dakota	2.24	1.71	1.86	1.21

TABLE G.1
Measures of State Accountability and NAEP vs. State Assessment Discrepancies in Reading and Math Proficiency (continued)

State	Ratio of State Assessment to NAEP Proficiency			
	Grade 4		Grade 8	
	Reading	Math	Reading	Math
Ohio	2.06	1.58	2.45	2.1
Oklahoma	2.83	3.39	2.74	3.85
Oregon	2.74	2.7	1.69	1.83
Pennsylvania	1.72	1.62	1.81	1.86
Rhode Island	2.05	1.55	1.43	1.5
South Carolina	1.28	1.2	1	0.97
South Dakota	2.61	2.07	2.13	1.76
Tennessee	—	—	—	—
Texas	3.11	3.03	3.14	3.17
Utah	2.43	2.33	2.12	1.91
Vermont	2.13	1.74	1.59	1.91
Virginia	2.25	2.25	1.95	2.41
Washington	1.99	1.49	1.47	1.28
West Virginia	—	—	—	—
Wisconsin	2.45	2.09	2.14	1.86
Wyoming	1.36	0.95	1.2	1.09

TABLE G.2
Correlations of State Accountability Variable with the NAEP vs. State Assessment Discrepancies in Proficiency Levels and Gaps by Grade and Subject

	Grade 4		Grade 8	
	Reading	Math	Reading	Math
All	.13	.31**	.17	.36**
White	−.02	.13	.05	.26*
Black	.15	.30*	.13	.32*
Hispanic	.02	.08	.14	.25
Asian	−.30*	−.33*	−.11	−.02
Nonpoor	−.07	−.12	−.00	.02
Poor	.20	.24	.29*	.35**
White–Black gap	−.27**	−.34**	−.14	−.36**
White–Hispanic gap	.02	−.03	−.07	−.10
Poverty gap	−.17	−.14	−.07	−.11

Note. The above correlation coefficients show the direction and strength of linear relationship between two variables: (1) the level of state activism in test-driven accountability and (2) the size of discrepancies between NAEP and state assessment in proficiency rate. Positive values mean the variables change in the same direction, whereas negative values mean they change in the opposite direction. Asterisks indicate statistical significance level of the correlation estimate: * $p < .05$; ** $p < .01$.

TABLE G.3
State Assessment vs. NAEP Discrepancies in 2003–05 Proficiency Gain by Grade and Subject (N = 25 states)

	State Assessment			NAEP		
	2003 % at/above Proficient	2005 % at/above Proficient	2003–05 % Gain	2003 % at/above Proficient	2005 % at/above Proficient	2003–05 % Gain
Grade 4						
Reading	66.6	71.8	+5.2	30.3	30.6	+0.3
Math	61.4	67.4	+6	31.6	36.1	+4.5
Grade 8						
Reading	63.1	66.6	+3.5	31.2	29.7	−1.5
Math	48.8	56.0	+7.2	28.8	27.9	−0.9

REFERENCES

Adams, J. E., & Kirst, M. W. (1999). New demands and concepts for educational accountability: Striving for results in an era of excellence. In J. Murphy & K. S. Louis (Eds.), *Handbook of research on educational administration* (pp. 463–490). San Francisco: Jossey-Bass.

Ad Hoc Committee on Confirming Test Results. (2002, March 1). *Using the national assessment of educational progress to confirm state test results: A report of the Ad Hoc Committee on confirming test results.* Washington, DC: National Assessment Governing Board. Retrieved December 19, 2005, from http://nagb.org

Allen, N. L., Carlson, J.E. , & Zelenak, C.A. (1999). *The NAEP 1996 technical report.* Proportion of variance due to student sampling. This corresponds to reliability coefficient in classical test theory. Maine Department of Education (1995).

American Educational Research Association, American Psychological Association, & National Council on Educational Measurement. (1999). *Standards for educational and psychological testing.* Washington, DC: AERA.

American Institutes for Research. (2006, April). No Child Left Behind in 2004: Results from the National Longitudinal Study of NCLB and Study of State Implementation of NCLB. Symposium papers presented at the annual meeting of American Educational Research Association, San Francisco, CA.

Amrein, A. L. & Berliner, D.C. (2002, March 28). High-stakes testing, uncertainty, and student learning *Education Policy Analysis Archives, 10*(18). Retrieved June 14, 2003, from http://epaa.asu.edu/epaa/v10n18/.

Amrein-Beardsley, A. A., & Berliner, D.C. (2003, August 4). Re-analysis of NAEP math and reading scores in states with and without high-stakes tests: Responses to Rosenshine. *Education Policy Analysis Archives, 11*(25). Retrieved August 24, 2003, from http://epaa.asu.edu/epaa/v11n25/

Archbald, D. A., & Porter, A. C. (1994). Curriculum control and teachers' perceptions of autonomy and satisfaction. *Educational Evaluation and Policy Analysis, 16*(1), 21–39.

Baker, E. L. (2003). Multiple measures: Toward tiered systems. *Educational Measurement: Issues and Practice, 22*(2), 13–17.

Baker, D. P (2003). Should we be more like them? Reflections on causes of cross-national high school achievement differences and implications for American educational reform policy. In D. Ravitch (Ed.), *Brookings papers on education policy* (pp. 309–325). Washington DC: Brookings Institution.

Bartman, K. D. (2002). Public education in the 21st century: How do we ensure that no child is left behind? *Temple Political & Civil Rights Law Review, 12*(1), 95–119.

Barton, P. E. (2002). *Raising achievement and reducing gaps: Reporting progress toward goals for academic achievement in mathematics.* Washington, DC: National Education Goals Panel.

Barr, R., & Dreeben, R. (1983). *How schools work.* Chicago: University of Chicago Press.

Barr, R., & Dreeben, R. (1988). The formation and instruction of ability groups. *American Journal of Education, 97*(1), 34–64.

Benveniste, G. (1985). The design of school accountability systems. *Educational Evaluation and Policy Analysis, 7*(3), 261–279.

Berliner, D. C., & Biddle, B. J. (1995). *The manufactured crisis: Myth, fraud, and the attack on America's public schools.* Reading, MA: Addison-Wesley.

Bidwell, C. E. (1965). The school as a formal organization. In J. G. March (Ed.), *Handbook of organizations.* Chicago: Rand-McNally.

Bishop, J. (2001). A steeper, better road to graduation. *Education Next.* Retrieved October 6, 2005, from http://www.educationnext.org/20014/index.html

Bishop, J. H., Mane, F., Bishop, M., & Moriarty, J. (2001). The role of end-of-course exams and minimum competency exams in standards-based reforms. In D. Ravitch (Ed.), *Brookings papers on education policy* (pp. 267–330). Washington, DC: Brookings Institution Press.

Blank, R. K., & Dalkilic, M. (1992). *State policies on science and mathematics education.* Washington DC: Council of Chief State School Officers. (ERIC Document Reproduction Service No. ED 350 163).

Bracey, G. W. (2002). Standards and Achievement Gaps. *Phi Delta Kappan, 83*(8), 643.

Braun, H. (2004). Reconsidering the impact of high-stakes testing. *Education Policy Analysis Archives, 12*(1). Retrieved March 10, 2004, from http://epaa.asu.edu/epaa/v12n1/.

Braun, H. I., Wang, A., Jenkins, F., & Weinbaum, E. (2006). The Black–White achievement gap: Do state policies matter? *Education Policy Analysis Archives, 14*(8). Retrieved May 1, 2006, from http://epaa.asu.edu/epaa/v14n8/.

Bryk, A. S., & Raudenbush, S. W. (1992). *Hierarchical linear models.* Newbury Park, CA: Sage.

Bryk, A., Thum, Y., Easton, J., & Luppescu, S. (1998). Assessing school academic productivity: The case of Chicago school reform. *Social Psychology of Education, 2*, 103.

Campbell, D. T., & Kenny, D. A. (1999). *A primer on regression artifacts.* New York: Guilford Press.

Campbell, D. T., & Stanley, J. C. (1963). *Experimental and quasi-experimental designs for research.* Chicago: Rand McNally.

Carey, K. (2004). *The funding gap 2004*. A report of the Education Trust. Retrieved March 10, 2006, from http://www.edtrust.org

Carnoy, M., & Loeb, S. (2002). Does external accountability affect student outcomes? *Educational Evaluation and Policy Analysis, 24*(4), 305–331.

Carnoy, M., Loeb, S., & Smith, T. (2001). *Do higher scores in Texas make for better high school outcomes?* (CPRE Research Report No. RR-047). Philadelphia, PA: Consortium for Policy Research in Education.

Cawelti, G. (2001). *High student achievement: How six school districts changed into high-performance systems.* Arlington, VA: Education Research Service.

Ceci, S. J., & Papierno, P. B. (2005). The rhetoric and reality of gap closing: When the "have-nots" gain but the "haves" gain even more. *American Psychologist, 60,* 149–160.

Center on Education Policy. (2006). *From the capital to the classroom: Year 4 of the No Child Left Behind Act.* Retrieved on May 15, 2006, from http://www.cep-dc.org

Clotfelter, C. T., & Ladd, H. (1996). Recognizing and rewarding success in public schools. In H. Ladd (Ed.), *Holding schools accountable* (pp. 23–64). Washington, DC: Brookings Institution Press.

Clotfelter, C. T., Ladd, H., Vigdor, J., & Aliago, R. (2004). *Teacher quality and minority achievement gaps.* Working paper series. SAN04-04 Duke University, Durham, NC: Terry Sanford Institute of Public Policy.

Cohen, D. K. (1990). A revolution in one classroom: The case of Mrs. Oublier. *Educational Evaluation and Policy Analysis, 12,* 311–329.

Cohen, D. K., & Haney, W. (1980). Minimums, competency testing, and social policy. In R.M. Jaeger & K.T. Carol (Eds.), *Minimum competency achievement testing* (Ch. 1). Berkeley, CA: McCutchan.

Cohen, D., Raudenbush, S., & Ball, D. (2003). Resources, instruction, and research. *Educational Evaluation and Policy Analysis, 25*(2), 119–142.

Coladarci, T. (2003). *Gallup goes to school: The importance of confidence intervals for evaluating "Adequate Yearly Progress" in small schools.* Washington, DC: Rural School and Community Trust Policy Brief.

Coleman, J. S., Campbell, E. Q., Hobson, C. J., McPartland, J., Mood, A. M., Weinfeld, A. D., & York, R. L. (1966). *Equality of educational opportunity.* Washington, DC: U.S. Government Printing Office.

Commission on Instructionally Supportive Assessment. (2001). *Building tests that support instruction and accountability: A guide for policymakers.* Washington, DC: Author.

Council of Chief State School Officers. (1996). *Key state education policies on K–12 education.* Washington, DC: Author.

Cuban, L. (1984). *How teachers taught.* New York: Longman.

Cuban, L. (1992). What happens to reforms that last?: The case of the junior high school. *American Educational Research Journal. 29*(2), 227–251.

Danzberger, J. P. et al. (1992). *Governing public schools: New times, new requirements.* Washington, DC: Institute for Educational Leadership.

Darling-Hammond, L. (1989). Accountability for professional practice. *Teachers College Record, 91,* 59–80.

Darling-Hammond, L., & Post, L. (2000). Inequality in teaching and schooling: Supporting high-quality teaching and leadership in low-income students. In R. D. Kahlenberg (Ed.), *A nation at risk* (pp. 127–168). New York: Century Foundation.

Davis, M. R. (2006, June 21). Ed. Dept. to weigh NCLB subgroup issues. *Education Week.* Retrieved November 8, 2006, from http://www.edweek.org.

DiMaggio, P. J., and Powell, W. W. (1991). The iron cage revisited: Institutional isomorphism and collective rationality. In W. W. Powell & P. J. DiMaggio (Eds.), *The new institutionalism in organizational analysis.* Chicago: University of Chicago Press.

Dorn, S. (1998). The political legacy of school accountability systems. *Education Policy Analysis Archives, 6*(1). Retrieved November 5, 2003, from http://epaa.asu.edu/epaa/v6n1

Eckstein, M. A., & Noah, H. J. (1993). *Secondary school examinations: International perspectives on policies and practices.* New Haven, CT: Yale University Press.

Education Trust. (2004). *Measured progress: Achievement rises and gaps narrow, but too slowly.* Washington, DC: Author.

Education Trust. (2006). *Primary progress, secondary challenge: A State-by-state look at student achievement patterns.* Washington, DC: Author.

Education Week. (March 17, 1993). Taking account: states move from "inputs" to "outcomes" in effort to regulate schools. Retrieved on May 10, 2003 from http://www.edweek.org.

Elmore, R. F. (1976). Follow through planned variation. In W. Williams & F. Elmore (Eds.), *Social program implementation.* New York: Academic Press.

Elmore, R. F. (1995). Teaching, learning, and school organization: Principles of practice and the regularities of schooling. *Educational Administration Quarterly, 31*(3), 355–374.

Elmore. R. F. (2002). Testing trap. *Harvard Magazine* Forum, September-October. Retrieved May 31, 2006 from www.harvard-magazine.com.

Elmore, R. F., & Fuhrman, S. (1995). Opportunity-to-learn standards and the state role in education. *Teachers College Record, 96,* 432–457.

Epstein, J. L., Herrick, S. C., & Coates, L. (1996). Effects of summer home learning packets on student achievement in language arts in the middle grades. *School Effectiveness and School Improvement, 7,* 383–410.

Erpenbarch, W. J., Forte-Fast, E., & Potts, A. (2003). *Statewide educational accountability under NCLB: Central issues arising from an examination of state accountability workbooks and U.S. Department of Education reviews under the No Child Left Behind Act of 2001.* Washington, DC: Council of Chief State School Officers.

FairTest. (2005, October 19). Flatline NAEP scores show failure of test-driven school reform: "No Child Left Behind" has not improved academic performance. Press release. Retrieved on May 15, 2006, from http://www.fairtest.org

Ferguson, R. (1991). Paying for public education: New evidence on how and why money matters. *Harvard Journal of Legislation, 28,* 465–498.

Ferguson, R., & Ladd, H. F. (1996). How and why money matters: An analysis of Alabama schools. In H. Ladd. (Ed.), *Holding schools accountable* (pp. 265–298). Washington, DC: Brookings Institution.

Finn, C. E., & Kanstoroom, M. (2001). State academic standards. In D. Ravitch (Ed.), *Brookings papers on education policy* (pp. 131–180). Washington, DC: Brookings Institution Press.

Fiske, E., & Ladd, H. (2000). *When schools compete: A cautionary tale.* Washington, DC: Brookings Institution Press.

Frederiksen, N. (1994). *The influence of minimum competency tests on teaching and learning*. Princeton, NJ: Educational Testing Service.

Fuhrman, S. H., (1988). State politics and educational reform. In S. H. Fuhrman et al. (Eds.), *Politics of reforming school administration*. London: Falmer Press.

Fuhrman, S. H. (1999). *The new accountability* (CPRE Policy Brief Series RB-27). Philadelphia, PA: University of Pennsylvania, Consortium for Policy Research in Education.

Fuller, B., Gesicki, K., Kang, E. & Wright, J. (2006). *Is the No Child Left Behind Act working?: The reliability of how states track achievement*. University of California, Berkeley PACE Working paper 06-1.

Gamoran, A., & Dreeben, R. (1986). Coupling and control in educational organizations. *Administrative Science Quarterly, 31*, 612–632.

Gardner, J. W. (1984). *Excellence: Can we be equal and excellent too*. New York: W. W. Norton & Company.

Ginsberg, R., & Wimpelberg, R. K. (1987). Educational change by commission: Attempting "trickle down" reform. *Educational Evaluation and Policy Analysis, 9*(4), 344–360.

Goertz, M.E. (1986). *State educational standards: A 50-State survey*. Princeton, NJ: ETS. (ERIC Document Reproduction Service No. ED 275 726).

Goertz, M. E., & Duffy, M. E. (2001). *Assessment and accountability systems in the 50 states: 1999–2000* (CPRE Research Report RR-046). Philadelphia, PA: Consortium for Policy Research in Education.

Goertz, M. E., & Duffy, M. E. (2001). *Assessment and accountability systems in the 50 states: 1999–2000* (CPRE Research Report RR-046). Philadelphia, PA: Consortium for Policy Research in Education.

Green, T. F. (1982). Excellence, equity, and equality. In L. S. Shulman and G. Sykes (Eds.), *The handbook on teaching and policy*. New York: Longman.

Grissmer, D., & Flanagan, A. (1998). *Exploring rapid achievement gains in North Carolina and Texas*. Washington, DC: National Education Goals Panel.

Grissmer, D., Flanagan, A., Kawata, J., & Williamson, S. (2000). *Improving student achievement: What state NAEP test scores tell us*. Santa Monica, CA: Rand.

Hall, D., & Kennedy, S. (2006). *Primary progress, secondary challenge*. A report of the Education Trust. Retrieved March 30, 2006, from http://www.edtrust.org

Haney. W. (2000). The myth of the Texas miracle in education. *Educational Policy Analysis Archives*. Retrieved March 3, 2001, from http://epaa.asu.edu/epaa/v8n41

Hanushek, E. A. (1994). A jaundiced view of 'adequacy' in school finance reform. *Educational Policy, 8*(4), 460–469.

Hanushek, E. A. (1997). Assessing the effects of school resources on student performance: An update. *Educational Evaluation and Policy Analysis, 19*, 141–164.

Hanushek, E. A., & Raymond, M. E. (2004). Does school accountability lead to improved performance? *Journal of Policy Analysis and Management, 24*(2), 297-327.

Harris, D. N., & Herrington, C. D. (2006). Accountability, standards, and the growing achievement gap: Lessons from the past half-century. *American Journal of Education, 112*, 209–238.

Hedges, L. V. (1990). Directions for future methodology. In K. W. Watcher & M. L. Straf (Eds.), *The future of meta-analysis* (pp. 11–26). New York: Russell Sage Foundation.

Hedges, L. V., Laine, R. D., & Greenwald, R. (1994). Does money matter? A meta-analysis of studies of the effects of differential school inputs on student outcomes. *Educational Researcher, 23*(3), 5–14.

Henderson-Montero, D., Julian, M. W., & Yen, W. M. (2003). Multiple measures: Alternative design and analysis models. *Educational Measurement: Issues and Practice, 22*(2), 7–12.

Heubert, J. P. (2000). Graduation and promotion testing: Potential benefits and risks for minority students, English-language learners, and students with disabilities. *Poverty and Race, 9*(5), 1–2, 5–7.

Hill, R. (1997). *Calculating and reducing errors associated with the evaluation of adequate yearly progress.* Paper presented at the annual assessment conference of the CCSSO. (ERIC Publication No. ED 414307).

Hill, R. (2001, October). *Issues related to the reliability of school accountability scores.* Paper presented at the Reidy Interactive Lecture Series, Nashua, NH.

Hoff, D. J. (2006, November 8). Education dept. poised to approve more states for growth-model pilot. *Education Week.* Retrieved November 8, 2006, from http://www.edweek.org.

Hoxby, C. M. (2002). *The cost of accountability* (National Bureau of Economic Research Working Paper 8855). Retrieved September 10, 2003, from http://www.nber.org/papers/w8855

Husén, T., & Tuijnman, A. (1994). Monitoring standards in education: Why and how it came about. In A. Tuijnman & T. N. Postlethwaite (Eds.), *Monitoring the standards of education* (pp. 1–21). Oxford: Pergamon.

Ingersoll, R. (1996). The problem of under-qualified teachers in American secondary schools. *Educational Researcher, 28*(2), 26–37.

Jackson, P. (1968). *Life in classrooms.* New York: Holt, Rinehart and Winston.

Jacob, B. A. (2001). Getting tough? The impact of high school graduation exams. *Educational Evaluation and Policy Analysis, 23*(2), 99–121.

Jencks, C., & Phillips, M. (Eds.). (1998). *The Black–White test score gap.* Washington, DC: Brookings Institution Press.

Jerald, C. D. (2002). *All talk, no action: Putting an end to out-of-field teaching.* A report of the Education Trust. Retrieved March 10, 2006, from http://www.edtrust.org

Jordan, K., & McKeown, M. P. (1990). State fiscal policy and education reform. in J. Murphy (Ed.) *The education reform movement of the 1980s: Perspectives and cases* (pp. 90–123). Berkeley, CA: McCutchan.

Kaestle, C. F. (1985). Education reform and the swinging pendlum. *Phi Delta Kappan, 66,* 422–423.

Kaestle, C. F. (1993). The awful reputation of educational research. *Educational Researcher, 22*(1), 26–31.

Kane, T. J., & Staiger, D. O. (2002). Volatility in school test scores. In D. Ravitch (Ed.), *Brookings papers on education policy 2002* (pp. 235–284). Washington, DC: Brookings Institution.

Kelley, C., Heneman, H., & Milanowski, A. (2000). *School-based performance award programs, teacher motivation, and school performance: Findings from a study of three programs* (CPRE Research Report RR-44). Philadelphia, PA: Consortium for Policy Research in Education.

Kentucky Department of Education. (1997). KIRIS accountability cycle 2 technical manual.

Kentucky Department of Education. (2004). *Kentucky's Consolidated State Application, Revised Accountability Workbook, June 15, 2004.* Retrieved on May 16, 2005 from http://www.education.ky.gov.

Kim, J., & Sunderman, G. L. (2004). *Large mandates and limited resources: State response to the No Child Left Behind Act and implications for accountability.* Cambridge, MA: The Civil Rights Project at Harvard.

Klein, S. P., Hamilton, L.S., McCaffrey, D. F., & Stecher, B. M. (2000). *What do test scores in Texas tell us?* Santa Monica, CA: Rand.

Koretz, D. (2003). Using multiple measures to address perverse incentives and score inflation. *Educational Measurement: Issues and Practice, 22*(2), 18–26.

Koretz, D., & Barron, S. I. (1998). *The validity of gains on the Kentucky Instructional Results Information System (KIRIS)* (MR-792-PCT/FF). Santa Monica, CA: Rand.

Langenfeld, K. L., Thurlow, M. L., & Scott, D. L. (1996). *High stakes testing for students: Unanswered questions and implications for students with disabilities* (Synthesis Report No. 26). Minneapolis, MN: University of Minnesota, National Center on Educational Outcomes. Retrieved January 10, 2005, from http://education.umn.edu/NCEO/OnlinePubs/Synthesis26.htm

Lee, J. (1997). State activism in education reform: Applying the Rasch model to measure trends and examine policy coherence. *Educational Evaluation and Policy Analysis, 19*(1), 29–43.

Lee, J. (1998a). State policy correlates of the achievement gap among racial and social groups. *Studies in Educational Evaluation, 24*(2), 137–152.

Lee, J. (1998b). The impact of content-driven state education reform on instruction. *Research in Middle Level Education Quarterly, 21*, 15–29.

Lee, J. (1998c). *Assessing the Performance of Public Education in Maine: Factors Influencing School Differences.* Occasional Paper No. 29. Orono, ME: University of Maine Center for Research and Evaluation.

Lee, J. (2001). School reform initiatives as balancing acts: Policy variation and educational convergence among Japan, Korea, England and the United States. *Educational Policy Analysis Archives.* Retrieved October 10, 2005, from http://epaa.asu.edu/epaa/v9n13.html.

Lee, J. (2002). Racial and ethnic achievement gap trends: Reversing the progress toward equity? *Educational Researcher, 31*(1), 3–12.

Lee, J. (2003). Evaluating rural progress in mathematics achievement: Threats to the validity of "Adequate Yearly Progress." *Journal of Research in Rural Education, 18*, 67–77.

Lee, J. (2004a). Evaluating the effectiveness of instructional resource allocation and use: IRT and HLM Analysis of NAEP teacher survey and student assessment data. *Studies in Educational Evaluation, 30*, 175–199.

Lee, J. (2004b). How feasible is Adequate Yearly Progress (AYP)? Simulations of school AYP "Uniform Averaging" and "Safe Harbor" under the No Child Left

Behind Act. *Education Policy Analysis Archives* [Online], *12*(14). Retrieved January 10, 2005 from http://epaa.asu.edu/epaa/v12n14/.

Lee, J. (2004c). Multiple facets of inequity in racial and ethnic achievement gaps. *Peabody Journal of Education, 79*(2), 51–73.

Lee, J. (2006a). *Tracking achievement gaps and assessing the impact of NCLB on the gaps: An in-depth look into national and state reading and math outcome trends.* Cambridge, MA: The Civil Rights Project at Harvard University.

Lee, J. (2006b). Input-guarantee vs. performance-guarantee approaches to School accountability: Cross-state comparisons of policies, resources, and outcomes. *Peabody Journal of Education, 81*(4), 43–64.

Lee, J. (2007). State report card on educational equity: Racial and socioeconomic segregations, inequalities, and achievement Gaps. In J. Lee (Ed.). *How national data help tackle the achievement gap* (pp. 53–70). Buffalo, NY: SUNY Buffalo Graduate School of Education Publications.

Lee, J. (in press). Do national and state assessments converge for educational accountability? A meta-analytic synthesis of multiple measures in Maine and Kentucky. *Applied Measurement in Education.*

Lee, J., & Coladarci, T. (2002). *Using multiple measures to evaluate the performance of students and schools: Learning from the cases of Kentucky and Maine.* Orono: University of Maine.

Lee, J., & McIntire, W. (2002). *Using national and state assessments to evaluate the performance of state education systems: Learning from the cases of Kentucky and Maine.* Orono: University of Maine.

Lee, J., & Wong, K. K. (2004). The impact of accountability on racial and socioeconomic equity: Considering both school resources and achievement outcomes. *American Educational Research Journal, 41*(4).

Lee, V. E., & Smith, J. B. (1999). Social support and achievement for young adolescents in Chicago: The role of school academic press. *American Educational Research Journal, 36*(4), 907–945.

LeFloch, K. C., Taylor, J., & Thomsen, K. (2006, April). *The implications of NCLB accountability for comprehensive school reform.* Paper presented at the annual meeting of American Educational Research Association.

Leithwood, K., Steinbach, R., & Jantzi, D. (2002). School leadership and teachers' motivation to implement school accountability policies. *Educational Administration Quarterly, 38*(1), 94–119.

Levin, B. (2001). *Reforming education: From origins to outcomes.* London: Routledge-Falmer.

Linn, R. L. (2000). Assessments and accountability. *Educational Researcher, 2*(29), 4–16.

Linn, R. L. (2003). Accountability: Responsibility and reasonable expectations. *Educational Researcher, 32*(7), 3–13.

Linn, R. L., Baker, E. L., & Betebenner, D. W. (2002). Accountability systems: Implications of requirements of the No Child Left Behind Act of 2001. *Educational Researcher, 31*, 3–16.

Linn, R. L., & Gronlund, N. E. (2000). *Measurement and assessment in teaching* (8th ed.). Englewood Cliffs, NJ: Prentice-Hall.

Linn, R. L., & Haug, C. (2002). Stability of school-building accountability scores and gains. *Educational Evaluation and Policy Analysis, 24*(1), 29–36.

Linton, T. H., & Kester, D. (2003). Exploring the achievement gap between white and minority students in Texas: A comparison of the 1996 and 2000 NAEP and TAAS eighth grade mathematics test results. *Education Policy Analysis Archives, 11*(10). Retrieved May 1, 2006, from http://epaa.asu.edu/epaa/v11n10/

Lortie, D. C. (1975). *Schoolteacher: A sociological study.* Chicago: University of Chicago Press.

Loveless, T. (1993). Organizational coupling and the implementation of tracking reform. *Administrator's Notebook, 35*(8).

Loveless, T. (2006). *How well are American students learning?* Brown Center Report on American Education, Volume II, Number 1. Washington, DC: Brookings Institution.

Lubienski, S. T. (2006). Examining instruction, achievement, and equity with NAEP mathematics data. *Education Policy Analysis Archives, 14*(14). Retrieved July 3, 2006, from http://epaa.asu.edu/epaa/v14n14/.

MacQuarrie, D. (2002, September). The No Child Left Behind Act: Regulatory guidance. *NCME Newsletter, 10*(3), 3–4.

Madaus, G. (1988). The influence of testing on the curriculum. In L. Tanner (Ed.), *Critical issues in curriculum: 87th yearbook of the NSSE Part 1.* Chicago: University of Chicago Press. (ERIC Document Reproduction Service No. 263 183).

Maine Department of Education. (1995). *Maine Educational Assessment 1994–95 Questions and Answers.* Augusta, ME: Author.

Maine Department of Education. (2003). *The federal "No Child Left Behind" Act: Understanding Adequate Yearly Progress Fact Sheet.* Retrieved on May 16, 2005 from http://www.maine.gov/education.

Marion, S. F., White, C., Carlson, D., Erpenbach, W. J., Rabinowitz, S., & Sheinker, J. (2002). *Making valid and reliable decisions in the determination of adequate yearly progress.* A Paper in the Series: Implementing The State Accountability System Requirements Under the No Child Left Behind Act of 2001. Washington, DC: Council of Chief State School Officers.

Mathis, W. J. (2003). No Child Left Behind: Costs and benefits. *Phi Delta Kappan, 84*(9), 679–686. Retrieved 16 March, 2003 from http://www.pdkintl.org/kappan/k0305mat.htm

McAdams, D. R. (2000). *Fighting to save our urban schools . . . and winning: Lessons from Houston.* New York: Teachers College Press.

McDonnell, L. M., & Elmore, R. F. (1987). Getting the job done: Alternative policy instruments. *Educational Evaluation and Policy Analysis, 9,* 133–152.

McLaughlin, M. (1976). Implementation as mutual adaptation: Change in classroom organization. In W. Williams & F. Elmore (Eds.), *Social program implementation.* New York: Academic Press.

McLaughlin, M. (1991). Test-based accountability as a reform strategy. *Phi Delta Kappan, 73*(3). 248–251.

Meyer, J. W., & Rowan, B. (1978). The structure of educational organizations. In M. W. Meyer et al. (Eds.), *Environments and organizations.* San Francisco: Jossey-Bass.

Meyer, R. H. (1997). Value-added indicators of school performance: A primer. *Economics of Education Review, 16*(3), 283–301.

Mintrop, H. & Trujillo, T.M. (2005). Corrective action in low performing schools: Lessons for NCLB implementation from first-generation accountability systems. *Education Policy Analysis Archives, 13*(48). Retrieved December 15, 2005, from http://epaa.asu.edu/epaa/v13n48/

Mitchell, D. E., Roysdon, G. W., Wirt, F. M., & Marshall, C. (1990). The structure of state education policy. In P. W. Thurston & L. S. Lotto (Eds.), *Advances in educational administration* (Vol. 1, Part A, pp. 221–252). Greenwich, CT: JAI Press.

Mullis, I. V.S. et al. (1993). *NAEP 1992 mathematics report card for the nation and the states* (Report No. 23-ST02). Washington, DC: National Center for Education Statistics.

Murnane, R. (1975). *The impact of school resources on the learning of inner city children.* Cambridge, MA: Ballinger Publishing Co.

Murnane, R., & Levy, R. J. (1996). *Teaching the new basic skills.* New York: The Free Press.

Murphy, J. (1990). The education reform movement of the 1980s: A comprehensive analysis. In J. Murphy (Ed.), *The education reform movement of the 1980s: Perspectives and cases.* Berkeley, CA: McCutchan.

Murphy, J., Hallinger, P., & Mesa, R. P. (1985). School effectiveness: Checking progress and assumptions and developing a role for state and federal government. *Teachers College Record, 86*, 615–41.

Murray, C. (2006, July 25). Acid tests. *The Wall Street Journal.* Retrieved July 27, 2006, from http://www.opinionjournal.com.

Nathan, R.P. (1990). Federalism—The great composition. In A. King (Ed.), *The new American political system.* Washington, DC: The AEI Press.

NAACP. (2005). *Moving From rhetoric to reality in opening doors to higher education for African-American students.* New York: Author.

National Center for Education Statistics. (1996). *Pursuing excellence: A study of U.S. eighth-grade mathematics and science teaching, learning, curriculum, and achievement in international context.* Washington, DC: U.S. Department of Education, National Center for Education Statistics.

National Commission on Excellence in Education. (1983). *A nation at risk: The imperative for education reform.* Washington, DC: U.S. Government Printing Office.

National Research Council. (1999). *High stakes: Testing for tracking, promotion, and graduation.* In J. P. Heubert & R. M. Hauser (Eds.), *Committee on appropriate test use.* Washington, DC: National Academy Press.

National Research Council. (2002). *Scientific research in education.* In R.J. Shavelson & L. Towne (Eds.), *Committee on Scientific Principles for Education Research.* Washington, DC: National Academy Press.

National School Boards Association. (2006). *Federal funding for education.* Alexandria, VA: Author.

New England Center for Educational Policy and Leadership. (2002). *Implementing the No Child Left Behind Act of 2001: A tool kit for New England state policy makers.* Storrs, CT: Author.

Newmann, F. M., King, M. B., & Rigdon, M. (1997). Accountability and school performance: Implications from restructuring schools. *Harvard Educational Review, 67*(1), 41–74.

Newmann, F. M., & Wehlage, G. G. (1995). *Successful school restructuring.* Madison, WI: Center on Organization and Restructuring of Schools.

Nichols, S. L., Glass, G. V, & Berliner, D. C. (2006). High-stakes testing and student achievement: Does accountability pressure increase student learning? *Education Policy Analysis Archives, 14*(1). Retrieved May 1, 2006 from http://epaa.asu.edu/epaa/v14n1/.

No Child Left Behind Act of 2001, Pub. L. No. 107-110.

Noddings, N. (1992). Excellence as a guide to educational conversation. *Philosophy of Education Yearbook.* Retrieved May 10, 2006 from http://www.ed.uiuc.edu/EPS/PES-Yearbook/92_docs/Noddings.HTM

North Central Regional Education Laboratory/Council of Chief State School Officers. (1996). *State assessment program database.* Oak Brook, IL: NCREL.

O'Day, J. (2002). Complexity, accountability, and school improvement. *Harvard Educational Review, 72*(3).

O'Day, J., & Smith, M. (1993). Systemic reform and educational opportunity. In S. Fuhrman (Ed.), *Designing coherent educational policy* (Ch. 8). San Francisco: Jossey-Bass.

Olson, L. (2002, April 18). 'Inadequate' yearly gains are predicted. *Education Week.* Retrieved April 30, 2002, from http://www.edweek.org.

Olson, L. (2005a, November 30). State test programs mushroom as NCLB mandate kicks in. *Education Week.* Retrieved November 20, 2006, from http://www.edweek.org.

Olson, L. (2005b, November 30). Federal review puts state tests under scrutiny. *Education Week.* Retrieved November 20, 2006, from http://www.edweek.org.

Orfield, G., & Yun, J. T. (1999). *Resegregation in American schools.* Cambridge, MA: Harvard University Civil Rights Project.

Paik, S. J., & Phillips, R. (2002). Student mobility in rural communities:What are the implications for student achievement? NCREL report. Retrieved May 10, 2003, from http://www.ncrel.org.

Perie, M., Grigg, W., & Dion, G. (2005). *The nation's report card: Mathematics 2005.* (NCES 2006-453). U.S. Department of Education, NCES. Washington, DC: U.S. Government Printing Office.

Perie, M., Grigg, W., & Donahue, P. (2005). *The nation's report card: Reading 2005* (NCES 2006-451). U.S. Department of Education, NCES. Washington, DC: U.S. Government Printing Office.

Peterson, P. E. (1981). *City limits.* Chicago: The University of Chicago Press.

Peterson, P. E. (Ed.). (2006). *Generational change: Closing the test score gap.* Lanham, MD: Rowman & Littlefield.

Peterson, P. E., Rabe, B., & Wong, K. (1986). *When federalism works.* Washington, DC: Brookings Institution.

Phelps, R. (Ed.) (2005). *Defending standardized tests.* Mawah, NJ: Lawrence Erlbaum.

Phillips, G. W., & Adcock, E. P. (1997). *Measuring school effects with HLM: data handling and modeling issues.* Paper presented at the annual meeting of the AERA. (ERIC Document Reproduction Service No. ED 409 330).

Popham, J. W. (2004). *America's "failing" schools: How parents and teachers can cope with NCLB.* London: RoutledgeFalmer.

Porter, A. (2003, October). *Prospects for school reform and closing the achievement gap.* Paper presented at Educational Testing Service's Invitational Conference, "Measurement and Research Issues in a New Accountability Era", New York City.

Porter, A., & Chester, M. (2002). Building a high-quality assessment and accountability program: The Philadelphia example. In D. Ravitch (Ed.). *Brookings papers on education policy* (pp. 285–315). Washington DC: Brookings Institution.

Putnam, R. (1995). Bowling alone: America's declining social capital. *Journal of Democracy, 6*(1), 65–78.

Quality counts '99: Rewarding results, punishing failure. (1999, January). *Education Week.* Retrieved September 10, 2001, from *http://www.edweek.com*

Quality counts 2001: Better balance. (2001, January). *Education Week.* Retrieved September 10, 2001, from http://www.edweek.com

Raising the bar: The complexities of "adequate yearly progress." (2002). *Education Assessment Insider, 1*(5), 5.

Raudenbush, S. W. (2004). *Schooling, statistics, and poverty: Can we measure school improvement?* Angoff Lecture No. 9. Princeton, NJ: ETS.

Raudenbush, S. W., & Willms, J. D. (1995). The estimation of school effects. *Journal of Educational and Behavioral Statistics, 20*(4), 307–335.

Ravitch, D. (1995). *National standards and American education.* Washington, DC: Brookings.

Raymond, M. E., & Haushek, E. A. (2003). High-stakes research. *Education Next,* Summer/No.3. Retrieved January 20, 2004 from http://www.education-next.org.

Rebell, M. A. (2006). Adequacy cost studies: Perspectives on the state of the art. *Education Finance and Policy, 1*(4). 465–483.

Roderick, M., Bryk, A. S., Jocob, B. A., Easton, J. Q., & Allensworth, E. (1999). *Ending social promotion in Chicago.* Chicago: Consortium on Chicago School Research.

Roderick, M., & Engel, M. (2001). The grasshopper and the ant: Motivational responses of low-achieving students to high-stakes testing. *Educational Evaluation and Policy Analysis, 23*(3), 197–227.

Rosenshine, B. (2003, August 4). High-stakes testing: Another analysis. *Education Policy Analysis Archives, 11*(24). Retrieved December 8, 2004, from http://epaa.asu.edu/epaa/v11n24/.

Rothstein, R. (2004). *Class and schools: Using social, economic, and educational reform to close the Black–White achievement gap.* Washington, DC: Economic Policy Institute.

Rowan, B. (1982). Organizational structure and the institutional environment: The case of public schools. *Administrative Science Quarterly, 27,* 259–279.

Rowan, B. (1996). Standards as incentives for instructional reform. In S. H. Fuhrman & J. A O'Day (Eds.), *Rewards and reform.* San Francisco: Jossey-Bass.

Rowan, B., & Miskel, C. G. (1999). Institutional theory and the study of educational organizations. In J. Murphy & K. S. Louis (Eds.), *Handbook of research on educational administration* (pp. 359–384). San Francisco: Jossey-Bass.

Sanders, W., Saxton, A., & Horn, B. (1997). The Tennessee value-added assessment system: A quantitative outcomes-based approach to educational assessment. In J. Millman (Ed.), *Grading teachers, grading schools: Is student achievement a valid educational measure?* (pp. 137–162). Thousand Oaks, CA: Corwin Press.

Schafer, W. D. (2003). A state perspective on multiple measures in school accountability. *Educational Measurement: Issues and Practice, 22*(2), 27–31.

Schmidt, W. H., McKnight, C. C, & Raizen, S. A. (1997). *A Splintered vision: An investigation of U.S. science and mathematics education.* Dordrecht: Kluwer.

Shafritz, J. M., & Ott, J. S. (2001). *Classics of organization theory.* Belmont, MA: Wadsworth.

Shiller, K., & Mueller, C. (2003). Raising the bar and equity? Effects of state high school graduation requirements and accountability policies on students' mathematics course taking. *Educational Evaluation and Policy Analysis, 25*(3), 299–318.

Sirotnik, K. A. (Ed.). (2004). *Holding accountability accountable: What ought to matter in public education.* New York: Teachers College Press.

Skrla, L., & Scheurich, J. J. (2001). Displacing deficit thinking in school district leadership. *Education and Urban Society, 33*(3), 239–255.

Skrla, L., Scheurich, J. J., & Johnson, J. F. (2000). *Equity-driven, achievement-focused school districts.* Austin, TX: Charles A. Dana Center.

Skrla, L., Scheurich, J. J., Johnson, J. F., & Koschoreck, J. W. (2004). Accountability for equity: Can state policy leverage social justice? In L. Skrla & J. J. Scheurich (Eds.), *Educational equity and accountability: Paradigms, policies, and politics* (pp. 51–78). New York, NY: RoutledgeFalmer.

Slavin, R. E. (2002). Evidence-based education policies: Transforming educational practice and research. *Educational Researcher, 31*(7), 15–21.

Smith, M. L., Heinecke, W., & Noble, A. J. (1999). Assessment policy and political spectacle. *Teachers College Record, 101*(2), 157–191.

Smith, M. S., & O'Day J. A. (1991). Systemic school reform. In S. Fuhrman, & B. Malen (Eds.), *The politics of curriculum and testing.* Bristol, PA: Falmer Press.

Snow-Renner, R. & Torrence, M. (2002). *ESEA 2001 Policy Brief: State Information Systems.* Denver, Colorado: Education Commission of the States.

Sunderman, G. L., Kim, J. S., & Orfield, G. (2005). *NCLB meets school realities: Lessons from the field.* Thousand Oaks, CA: Corwin Press.

Swanson, C. B., & Stevenson, D. L. (2002). Standards-based reform in practice: Evidence on state policy and classroom instruction from the NAEP state assessments. *Educational Evaluation and Policy Analysis, 24*(1), 1–28.

Thum, Y. (2002). *Design of school performance and school productivity indicators: Measuring student and school progress with the California API.* Working draft.

Tomlinson, T. M., & Cross, C. T. (1991). Student effort: The key to higher standards. *Educational Leadership, 49*(1), 69–73.

Tyack, D. & Cuban, L. (1995). *Tinkering toward utopia: A century of public school reform.* Cambridge, MA: Harvard University Press.

Underwood, J. (1989). State legislative responses to educational reform literature. In P.W. Thurston & L.S. Lotto (Eds.), *Advances in educational administration* (Vol. 1, Part A, pp. 139–175). Greenwich, CT: JAI Press.

U.S. Department of Education. (2005). *The Achiever, 4*(12).

Valencia, R. R., Valenzuela, A., Sloan, K., & Foley, D. (2004). Let's treat the cause, not the symptoms: Equity and accountability in Texas revisited. In L. Skrla & J. J. Scheurich (Eds.), *Educational equity and accountability: Paradigms, policies, and politics* (Ch. 3, pp. 29–38). New York: RoutledgeFalmer.

Walberg, H. J. (2003). Accountability unplugged. *Education Next* (2). Retrieved January 20, 2004, from http://www.educationnext.org/20032/index.html

Wainer, H. (2004). Value-added assessment [special issue]. *Journal of Educational and Behavioral Statistics, 29*(1).

Weick, K. (1976). Educational organizations as loosely-coupled systems. *Administrative Science Quarterly, 21,* 1–16.

Weiss, H. B. (2005). Beyond the classroom: Complementary learning to improve achievement outcomes. *The Evaluation Exchange,* (11)1, 2–6.

West, M. R., & Peterson, P. E. (2005). *The efficacy of choice threats within school accountability systems: Results from legislatively induced experiments.* Paper presented at the Annual Conference of the Royal Economic Society, University of Nottingham.

Whang, P. A., & Hancock, G. R. (1994). Motivation and mathematics achievement: Comparisons between Asian-American and Non-Asian students. *Contemporary Educational Psychology, 19,* 302–322.

Wheat, D. (2000). *Value-added accountability: A systems solution to the school accreditation problem.* Thomas Jefferson Institute for Public Policy report. Retrieved January 20, 2001, from http://www.thomasjeffersoninst.org/pdfs/VAA_2nd_edition.pdf

Wilson, B. L., & Corbett, H. D. (1990). Statewide testing and local improvement: An oxymoron? In J. Murphy (Ed.), *The education reform movement of the 1980s: Perspectives and cases.* Berkeley, CA: McCutchan.

Wise, A. E. (1979). *Legislated learning: The bureaucratization of the American classroom.* Berkeley: University of California Press.

Wong, K. K. (1994). Bureaucracy and school effectiveness. *International Encyclopedia of education* (Vol. 6). *Educational Administration.*

Wong, K. K., & Lee, J. (1998). Interstate variation in the achievement gap among racial and social groups: Considering the effects of school resources and classroom practices. In K. K. Wong (Ed.), *Advances in Educational Policy* (Vol. 4, pp. 119–144). Greenwich, CT: JAI Press.

Yen, S., Schafer, W. D., & Rahman, T. (1999, April). School effect indices: stability of one- and two-level formulations. Paper presented at the annual meeting of the AERA (ERIC Document Reproduction Service No. ED 430 029).

Printed in the United States
85280LV00002B/290/A